LET LOVE BE GENUINE

Mental Handicap and the Church

Editor: Faith Bowers

The Baptist Union
London
1985

The Baptist Union
4 Southampton Row
London WC1B 4AB

LET LOVE BE GENUINE

(Romans 12 v. 9 RSV)

'The genuineness of love must include acceptance of what is genuinely there, as contrasted with what we simply imagine or wish to be there'.

Keith W. Clements
in *A Patriotism for Today*

CONTENTS

CONTRIBUTORS

Pat Battarbee# – Member, Tyndale Baptist Church, Bristol
Eileen Bebbington MA – Member, Stirling Baptist Church
Faith Bowers MPhil*# – Member, Bloomsbury Central Baptist Church
E. J. Clarke MA – Minister, West Watford Free Church
K. W. Clements MA BD – Tutor, Bristol Baptist College
Barbara Crowe MBE*# – Member, Avenue Baptist Church, Westcliff on Sea. Social worker to families with profoundly handicapped adults. Counsellor to parents of newly diagnosed handicapped babies
Trisha Dale MA* – Member, Blackheath and Charlton Baptist Church. Thesis on problems of parents with mentally handicapped children.
Jill Davis* RSCN – Member, Memorial Baptist Church, Plaistow
Brian Easter PhD, Dip.Theol., Dip.Past.Stud. – Full-time Anglican Chaplain to the Mental Handicap Units of the South Birmingham and Solihull Health Authorities (including Monyhull and Middlefield Hospitals)
Jean Forster – Member, Christ Church URC, Green End, Burnage
Gerald Forse – Minister, Chipping Norton Baptist Church
Marlene Fox ADSE* – Member, Leavesden Road Baptist Church, Watford. Deputy Headmistress, Breakspeare School, Abbots Langley
Bryan George BA* – Education Adviser, Baptist Union
Judy Martin – Member, Carshalton Beeches Baptist Free Church. Venture Scouts leader.
Edna Morgan# – Member, Christ Church URC, Green End, Burnage
Alastair Norris MA, Barrister-at-Law – Member, Haven Green Baptist Church, Ealing
George R. Neal BD# – Minister, Acocks-green Baptist Church, Birmingham
Frank Powell* RNMH, RMN, RGN – Member, Dagnall Street Baptist Church, St Albans. Chief Nursing Officer, Hertfordshire.
Rosemary Pratt# – Formerly at Carshalton Beeches Baptist Church, now in Kingaroy, Queensland, Australia
Tom Rogers – Secretary for Evangelism, Baptist Union
Marion Sadler# – Member, Christ Church, Painswick
Audrey Saunders SRN, RSCN*# – Member, New Road Church, Oxford
Barbara Stanford – Assistant Minister, Bloomsbury Central Baptist Church
Michael H. Taylor MA BD STM# – Director, Christian Aid. Formerly Principal, Northern Baptist College
Brian Windsor* IHSM, DHSA – Member, Four Oaks Baptist Church, Sutton Coldfield. Unit Administrator (Mental Handicap), North Warwickshire Health Authority. Formerly BMS (India) 1961-74

*   Denotes members of the Baptist Union Working Group on Mental Handicap and the Church
#   Denotes that a close relative is mentally handicapped

The Editor is also grateful to many others who have written or spoken to her. Their contributions, some of which are quoted, provide a basis in experience for the generalisations in her articles, and the substance of the unsigned articles.

FOREWORD

As the table of contents and the list of contributors in this book indicate, there is a widespread concern among Baptists about Christian ministry with the mentally handicapped. Some of that concern comes from families which face the reality of mental handicap within their own life. Other people have developed a keen interest because of their desire to help, and because they recognise the need for everyone, whatever their state of health, to live a meaningful life and grow to their full potential.

Baptists are by no means alone in this. But the working group which initiated this book has certainly pioneered in an area of church ministry not yet widely considered. As their work has become known other denominations have expressed encouragement and support. We congratulate the working group on their achievement.

Society as a whole needs to face the challenge of these pages. This is a comprehensive book with theological insight, relevance to many families and congregations, Christian compassion and a positive and creative spirit. I warm to the healthy partnership between church and secular disciplines and professions which it reveals. My hope is that the book will be read far beyond the Baptist family and that it will be used by God to stimulate new hope and purpose for many people.

Those who have contributed to the book will no doubt continue to express their concern in practical ways. They deserve both our gratitude and our prayers.

BERNARD GREEN

General Secretary,
Baptist Union of Great Britain & Ireland

INTRODUCTION

This book is the result of the inspiration and industry of the Baptist Union Working Group on Mental Handicap and the Church.

It is amazing what can be achieved in a short time by a group of dedicated people. September 1983 marked the beginning. Two friends called at the office to express concern about the way in which the church "accommodated" mentally handicapped people. Further, we realised that the current policy of closing hospitals and institutions and resettling the mentally handicapped in the community was likely to challenge many local fellowships. Could the Baptist Union help churches meet this situation?

An invitation was extended to all interested in or involved with the mentally handicapped in the church to come to a meeting at Bloomsbury Baptist Church. To our delight, this was not only well attended, but some had travelled from distant parts of the country. From among those present, a working group was formed: relatives of the handicapped, health service administrators, local church members and a teacher of severely handicapped children formed a balanced group.

During the last two years, needs have been assessed, places where work is already going on have been identified, resources have been catalogued and speakers provided for ministerial and lay training courses. In the summer of 1984 a series of articles in the *Baptist Times* disseminated information already collected. In this publication, we respond to the request to publish in a more permanent form. Other material collected since has been added.

Thanks are due to all who have contributed, to the Editor, Faith Bowers, and to Cathy Marsh and Carolyn Price for secretarial help.

BRYAN GEORGE

MENTAL HANDICAP - A DEFINITION

Mental handicap, which must not be confused with mental illness, is usually caused either by a genetic abnormality in a child, or by environmental factors arising during pregnancy, birth, or before the age of about 15 or 16 years when the genetically determined limits of intelligence are reached.

These environmental factors include maternal infection during pregnancy, infections during childhood and, occasionally, trauma at birth. Any of these may interfere with normal development. Accidents can also result in brain damage.

Epilepsy often accompanies the more severe degrees of mental handicap, and the various forms of mental illness can also occur amongst mentally handicapped people. Physical handicaps are often also present. Some conditions have a recognised collection of symptoms, like Down's Syndrome. Others are less clearly defined and development harder to predict.

Mental handicap does not respond to curative treatment as such, but much can be achieved by training in social functioning and self help skills to enable those concerned both to achieve and to extend their potential abilities, both practical and intellectual.

"I DON'T BELIEVE"

I don't believe I'm "meant" to be
The way I am.
I don't believe God muddled my genes
As part of His plan.

I don't believe His ears are deaf
To my poor speech.
I don't believe He withdraws his hand
From my short reach.

I don't believe He disregards
My mother's pain
As she sees me fail at a simple skill
Again and again.

I don't believe He especially chose
My family
To learn the harder lessons of life
Because of me.

I do believe God wants the best
In mind and form.
I won't blame Him that I've proved to be
Below the "norm".

I do believe that at my birth
God ached with grief,
As this time Nature got it wrong,
Bungled His brief.

I do believe that God is LOVE,
That Good must come,
As He helps me find my rightful place
In life and home.

Rosemary Pratt

Penned as if written by Jenny, her 9 year old daughter, who has Down's Syndrome. This poem appeared in the magazine of Carshalton Beeches Baptist Church, March 1985.

THE PASTORAL ROLE OF THE CHURCH

We readily acknowledge the direction to help the afflicted. When the afflicted in question are the mentally handicapped, it is important that we make a real effort to honour them – to respect them as men and women. This will colour how we help them, and how we accept their contribution to church and community life.

We look to the church as a caring community. We look to the minister, among other things, as pastor. Most ministers, learning of a baby born with mental handicap, of a child whose slow progress has at last been diagnosed as subnormal, of a youth who has suffered brain damage in an accident, would feel an early visit to the family was called for. Most would set out with sinking heart. What can Christians, individually and collectively, do to help the mentally handicapped and those who are close to them?

Many parents warmly acknowledge the supportive pastoral concern of their ministers and churches. Of course, those who did not experience this may not still be in the church to tell the tale. This must constantly be borne in mind when reading the 'good' examples cited in these pages. There can be few things sadder to hear than that a family went to church _until_ some disaster befell them. It does happen. Calamity can come upon Christian homes, and some fail to find in God their refuge and strength. This must not be forgotten as we hear how, for others, God has indeed 'sanctified to them their deepest distress'.

Churches do not always find it easy to accept the mentally handicapped. This is one problem which, if ignored, may well go away. Do we want the mentally handicapped and their families to go away from the church? If they are to be held and helped, the church must be sensitive to their real needs. The genuineness of love must embrace what is really there.

EARLY COUNSELLING

One of the most traumatic things that can happen in the life of a family is for a couple to be given a diagnosis of mental handicap for their newly born baby or small child. How that couple are given the news and what kind of counselling or help follows the diagnosis can make or mar the life of that family for many years to come.

The time at which that couple need help most is going to be at the time of diagnosis when the hurt is very deep. They will need a great deal of understanding and *em*pathy, not *sym*pathy, and a very positive approach from those around them. The church can play its part at this critical time.

It should be remembered that more or less every couple who give birth to a child with mental handicap will experience some form of rejection. It is not the child they are rejecting but all the unlooked for problems that they feel the handicap will create. They may wish their child had been still-born, that he might catch cold and die, or they may even be tempted to end the baby's life. Many people have been so tempted but have stopped themselves from taking such extreme action. If they have not reacted so strongly as this, they may still be asking the question 'Why us?' and they will be wondering 'How is this going to affect our future life together?' 'Can our marriage stand the extra stress and strain that will be placed upon it?' 'Can we cope?' 'What about our other children, how will they face up to having a mentally handicapped brother or sister?' 'What about the grandparents - will they think it is something we have done that has caused this?' 'What about the future, can we really face looking after a mentally handicapped adult?'

All very normal questions - but a couple may well develop quite a complex about their rejection. We all reject people or situations with which we find difficulty from time to time, but we accept that as being normal. However when parents reject a child for whom deep down they feel they should have extra love, then they feel guilty.

This rejection is often worse when it is experienced by a Christian couple. They and other Christians around them may well feel that their faith should uphold them, and when their very human misery takes over they feel an even greater sense of guilt.

It is important for anyone counselling such a couple to talk about rejection and assure them that it is a very normal thing to experience. They should explain at the outset that generally speaking it is nothing the parents have done that has caused this handicap, and of course many conditions (such as chromosome abnormalities) are determined at conception. Conception and birth is a miraculous process and occasionally all does not go well, but once the baby's condition is diagnosed then it is what is now made of the situation that is important. Most couples are going to feel at the outset that they cannot cope – this is often because they feel very alone and do not know who to turn to. It is important therefore that they should be assured they are not on their own, that they should be linked with other parents in a similar position (if they so wish) from as soon after the diagnosis is given them as is possible. They should be given information about services available; but always remember that any couple at this time will only take in a fraction of the information given them and much of it will need to be repeated several times.

The incidence of mental handicap is not uncommon and most churches will at some time have close contact with a child or adult with mental handicap and the family. It may well be that a Christian parent of a mentally handicapped child could be trained in counselling and could then be of service to others facing up to the situation for the first time. Churches should gather as much information as possible about local and national services to be in readiness, should a family come to their notice.

Parents often have great difficulty going on their own on their frequent visits to hospital, assessment centre, parent group meetings etc. A supportive friend from the church might be invaluable.

Always remember the super-sensitivity of parents. From the moment they are aware their child is different, they are conscious of the reactions of people around them. What is not said is often imagined and it is important that everyone remembers the importance of talking to a family with a handicapped child without embarrassment. To that family their child becomes important, and they need to share how they feel about him. All it needs is a friendly interest in how the child is progressing.

Never condemn if a family announces that they are going to give up their child. This decision will not have been taken lightly or easily, but it is not given to everyone to be able to give love to a child who is different. It shows a concern for the welfare of the child, if they feel they cannot give him love, to then decide their child should go to adoptive parents, who have love to give to a special child. In the 1980s there are a number of adoptive parents who have so much to give to a child with a handicap – much better than that that he should be denied the most important thing of all by his natural parents. But these parents are going to need a great deal of understanding and support if they are not to suffer guilt.

A test of how you should react to any parents, whatever the decisions they make about their handicapped child, is to try and imagine yourself in the same situation. How would you feel if you were told that the child, so long nurtured in the womb, for whom so many plans have been made, is mentally handicapped? You would wish for support, and hopefully you will be able to give it, should the opportunity come your way. You may then help a couple achieve the philosophy that my family reached many years ago, that it doesn't matter what Stephen cannot do, it is the special person he is, the way he makes everyone around him happy, and the many unexpected things he has achieved that are all important. What is normality anyway?

BARBARA CROWE

THE ONGOING SUPPORT OF FAMILIES

Parents of the mentally handicapped are hypersensitive. They live with strain and worry. They so often have to be on the defensive. Even those who appear to accept the situation well - and are admired for it - may remain sore and prickly underneath. We parents all *know* that everyone is sympathetic and means to be kind, but so often it is *we* who have to make allowances for those who, with well-meant clumsiness, say things that hurt. It seems a bit awry! My own bugbear is being told how loving and happy 'such children' are, how sweet and affectionate... So far I have resisted the temptation to offer condolences because the speaker has only been blessed with normal children...

It is not easy to advise on how to talk to parents, but perhaps venting some of the irritations parents usually try to keep to themselves may steer some kind friends away from the more unfortunate approaches.

Parents feel cut off, different from other families. It is hard to push your pram down the road and realise no-one wants to risk peeping at the new baby. Mental handicap scares people off. One mother describes taking her new baby, with Down's Syndrome, to church:

> After the initial adjustment which folk had to make (to be
> able to 'look' and not be afraid, and realise she was not
> just some monster), everyone accepted her extremely well.

7

When they grow older, isn't it hard to stop oneself looking twice at someone visibly peculiar? And hard then not to be embarrassed and turn quickly away if your sidelong glance was noticed?

It is not only emotional wear and tear that takes its toll on parents. A handicapped child is likely to be demanding. The worse the condition, the more exhausting for the parents, the greater the stress. Disturbed nights, frequent illness, incontinence, difficult behaviour are familiar to other parents, but in the handicapped they are more severe and go on for so much longer. You cannot tell yourself with certainty that 'he'll grow out of it'.

Many parents feel let down by the health services. The initial revelation is often badly handled. It is an awful thing to have to tell parents, but there are too many horror stories. Thereafter, too many parents find their child's handicap condemns them to repeated tussles with medical and social services. It should not be so. It is partly the result of the 'clinical approach', partly inevitable when case loads are too big to permit any real knowledge of the families, partly due to overstretched resources, partly to sheer insensitivity. Too often parents are treated as if they too are mentally defective - which can be jolly irritating! There are, of course, plenty of parents with happier experience. I have stressed the frequency of bad handling because, when doctors and social workers have done their worst, some parents will turn to the minister to pick up the pieces. I have done so myself. It may be hard to believe things have been managed so badly: the parents are distraught, so they probably exaggerate. They may not need to exaggerate.

Unhappy experiences may be a particular problem for middle class parents, who see doctors as their professional 'equals' and do not expect to be propped up by social workers, but all parents want to feel they and 'the experts' are pulling on the same side for the good of the child. No-one wants a battle where there should be co-operation. Where parents have to fight all along the line to get their child seen as an individual, not as a stereotype of his condition, it adds distressingly to their torment.

G.P.s often do not really know the families in their care. The minister can know people as people. He may therefore be better able to assess, through the immediate emotions, whether they are being unreasonable or not. That is a tough challenge. It can help.

Mental handicap is so hard to define, it is not surprising that most people have little understanding of it. We can imagine what it is like to be blind, or paralyzed, but it is almost impossible to imagine what it is like to be mentally handicapped. Anyway it is not a clear-cut state - there are many different types and levels of handicap.

People often ask, 'What is his mental age?' It is not that easy Development can be patchy. The ten year old may be like a seven year old in some respects, no more advanced than a three year old in others, yet in some ways seem fully up to his real age. I have watched my son turn to a small cousin for help with reading, and then take the little boy's hand protectively to see him across the road. You have to know the individual. This can present particular problems when trying to integrate the child with others, as in Sunday School.

In the book *Elizabeth Joy* (Lion 1984) Caroline Philps writes of some typical reactions to her daughter with Down's Syndrome:

> It has been hardest for me when people have not reacted at all... to have people react as if I'd said my daughter has a cold makes me feel I must be imagining the pain I feel.

She describes too the insensitivity of those who deny the condition, glibly assuring the mother 'she'll grow out of it'.

> There are other subtler forms of denial. People have said it is all a case of what we mean by 'normal'... Someone else suggested that no child is perfect... But there seems to me a difference between imperfections of little real consequence to one's expectations of life and something so fundamental which controls one's whole being.

Even within the Baptist Union Working Group I am gently reminded by my colleagues that I am 'fortunate', my son is on the 'upper end' of mental handicap, able to lead a relatively normal life. I recognise that, but at the same time want to cry out that he is still very handicapped. I watch him this year actually managing to write four or five consecutive, intelligible sentences - while his cousins of the same age have been deep in O levels. It still hurts.

The physical and mental strain on parents is great. When the handicap is severe, the demands are enormous. Even when the child is able to join in family life pretty well, that bit extra is called for, day in, day out. It has become clear that many can achieve more if there is enough stimulation. The various support bodies urge parents to follow careful programmes. It is good to feel there is something you can do to help your child develop. The handicapped *are* achieving more. And the parents constantly feel guilty that they never manage to do enough...

Then there are the policy questions. Should the child stay at home? Should he be put into care? What is the effect on other children in the family? What is best in education? If the child is relatively able, how much independence should be permitted? And, ever more insistently, what about the long-term future?

The mother especially can feel isolated from normal society. The father has less continual contact with the child, but the burden hovers constantly on his mind. Apart from the normal parental role, he needs to give extra support to his wife. The parents may grieve at the burden imposed on their other children, but they cannot take it away. It is not surprising that marriages often break under the strain.

Parents need to have some life of their own. They need a chance to be themselves, not just the parents of a handicapped child. They need time for their other children, to visit their schools, to take them out. Most parents know that in the early years with a normal child it is an effort to go out - to find a suitable babysitter, to get everything done in time, to have the energy left to enjoy an outing. With a handicapped child, things do not necessarily get easier with time. Parents may need a break but never get it. What life is like for those whose child is really difficult to manage, I can only begin to imagine. It is perhaps significant that the file of letters the Group has received from parents are almost all concerned with Down's Syndrome. The condition accounts for a high proportion of the mentally handicapped, but often the more manageable and educable. The parents of many with Down's Syndrome can write in about their child's acceptance within the church. Others too may be accepted - but their parents not have time to write.

At a party recently I watched three young people, all subnormal, all with different conditions. Two were able to merge in among the normal teenagers, helping themselves from the buffet, dancing and chatting in the garden. The third, severely handicapped, needed the full attention of both parents to keep her reasonably calm and quiet. They helped her eat a careful selection of non-messy food. It looked like handling an obstreperous toddler - but she was a young adult. Those of us nearby were carefully not being embarrassed. We 'understood'. The parents soon took her home. I can barely begin to understand what it is like to have a son or daughter like that.

Many parents are greatly helped by the various support groups run by Mencap, the Down's Childrens Association, and other bodies. If parents do not know what is available to them, the church might help find out and put them in touch. If, however, some parents are not drawn to these, they should not be made to feel guilty. Parents remain individuals with different tastes. Personally we avoided them, not wanting our lives dominated by mental handicap, and finding our 'support group' in our church. I found it more therapeutic to become a historian, which took me not 'out of myself' but rather out of the domestic round to territory where I could 'be myself'. I still feel a bit sheepish when people ask enthusiastically if I belong to DCA. Even for the many who welcome them, the support group meetings should not be the mother's only night out. People's tastes in escapism vary, but the parents of the mentally handicapped, with extra responsibilities and less of the joys of parenthood, need a chance to be themselves.

Parents are not the only relatives affected. Other members of the family, especially other children, will have their lives changed. Some brothers and sisters resent this and begrudge the time the parents are forced to give the handicapped child. This can lead to other problems. Many, however, accept the subnormal brother or sister remarkably well, perhaps more naturally than the parents ever can. Many parents would echo the appreciative comments of Rachel's mother, whose two elder daughters treated Rachel 'as a normal little girl, and when I once commented they replied "she is just our sister"'. Even so brothers and sisters are sometimes embarrassed, and as they get older may be troubled about the nature of handicap, why it happens, and whether there is a greater risk of their own children being defective. They may not want to burden their parents with their worries.

One remembers as a child thinking how left out her hyperactive, brain-damaged sister was, but also how demanding it was to look after her, even for a short time. In those days there was no school for her to attend and occasionally she would seek out big sister at school. She would 'burst into the classroom, and I still marvel that she knew exactly where to find me. At the time I was horrified, and wished that the ground would open and hide me for ever'. Yet she also remembers fighting another girl 'who called my sister a loony'. She goes on to make a telling comment:

> I was not aware at the time that we were restricted at home, although my parents felt that we were, and that we were unable to have friends home as often as they would have wished. It never occurred to me that my friends would not accept my sister.

Again it is this sister, rather than a parent, who reflects on another hurdle: 'I remember how we all dreaded her assessments because they emphasised the gulf that existed between her and the rest of us'.

My own elder son was shocked when I hesitated to take Richard to functions at his school. Again he assumed his friends would accept his brother - and they did. What troubled him more, when he was about ten, was the very good relationship between him and

Richard. We only realised this when they had been out with three teenagers, two brothers and a sister. Afterwards Keith told us with deep satisfaction, 'Those three really *like* each other. I am glad. Most of my friends fight their brothers and sisters. I didn't like to think Richard and I only get on well *because he isn't normal*'.

In these instances the normal siblings were older. It must be even harder when the younger, normal child is expected to keep a protective eye on the older, handicapped one. It should perhaps be added that the handicapped child, often imagined to be so free from baser emotions, is usually capable of jealousy, especially over claims on the mother's attention.

* * * * * * * * *

So what can the church do to help these families?

First, *cultivate positive attitudes*. People are instinctively repelled by mental handicap, but they can soon override that. Encourage people to welcome the child and take as near normal an interest as possible. Do not deny the abnormality, but don't keep on about it. Let the interest be in the child, in its pretty clothes or new toy even, rather than in the condition. If such an interest is maintained over the years, it will be very welcome.

Avoid sentimental, thoughtless kindness, even if it is the instinctive response. Kind remarks about 'such children' always being happy and loving, which sound so well-meaning and innocuous to others, can hurt parents. They hurt because they seem to deny the child's individuality, and because it is hard to have the more attractive aspects of your child written off as just part of his condition. Besides, mentally handicapped children - even those with Down's Syndrome - are not all happy and affectionate.

I remember for weeks after Richard's birth avoiding a close friend at church, because she would keep on about Richard's condition. It was kindly meant, but overwhelming. Another mother, probably embarrassed that she could find nothing to say, would squeeze my arm and talk about something quite different. I did not have to fight the tears with her, and I was grateful.

Pray. Sometimes prayer is the only possible help friends can give. Prayer can support, and can find a way through apparently insuperable problems. It is no good, however, just praying for the child to be cured. Prayer needs to be grounded in that love which recognises the facts of the situation and goes on from there. Such prayer may well prompt action.

Try to give practical help. Where the handicap is profound, the family may be virtually housebound. Friends are needed – friends to care, to listen, to help, to babysit long beyond infancy, perhaps just to watch over the handicapped child in another room and let the parents relax with their other children. Regular, reliable help, from people the handicapped child gets to know and trust, can make a great difference. This is something that the extended family of the church may be able to provide.

Even where the handicap is less severe, parents may find it hard to ask for sitters. Friends can help by offering to sit with the child – the teenager – the adult. The mother might welcome an occasional, unharassed shopping expedition. The parents might enjoy an outing on birthday or anniversary, even just a quiet walk in the sunshine. There may be a function at the other children's school. Perhaps they would love the chance to go quietly to church together.

Make them welcome. The more able mentally handicapped children of Christian families will probably be brought to church. Usually the crèche and Sunday School will accept them and cope with them as best they can. What about other youth activities? That will depend on local leaders and how much help they have. Where the mentally handicapped boy or girl can be included, it means a lot to them and their families. We have heard of a number of mentally handicapped children and teenagers enjoying Brownies, Scouts, Boys Brigade etc. Doubtless others could too. It is not always easy for parents to make the first approach: they know only too well that to include their child will mean extra work, extra responsibility for the leaders.

If the mentally handicapped child has grown up in the church, let them not be left out as they become older. The church should be alert to what they are capable of. Again parents may hesitate to make suggestions, but if asked probably know what their son or daughter could do 'properly'.

The criterion for church attendance is probably in practice socially acceptable behaviour. Even so, many of the mentally handicapped can behave 'acceptably', can worship with reverence. They can also enjoy socials and outings, and delight in little jobs for the church. Sometimes it is embarrassing. Their greetings can be so exuberant, their help so clumsy and slow, their conversation so hard to follow, so repetitive. If they are to be fully part of the fellowship, it will demand patience and tolerance. It will impose extra responsibility upon others. Where the church accepts this, it means so much.

The local church may be the only 'normal' community into which they are fully integrated. This helps to explain why not only Christ but His body, the Church, is so important in the lives of many handicapped people. Why I have heard my son singing in the bath, 'I like church, I do like church'. Why another mother can write:

> As for attending church, Joanne is always very keen, and if we are not going for some reason she wants to know why. I know she feels a real sense of belonging to the fellowship.

Other parents have written in this vein, but we must remember that they are the families who have been supported and have stayed in the church. Those who have left the church do not tell us of their experience. It is salutary therefore to quote another, older mother, with a more severely handicapped daughter. She writes 'of help so desperately needed and never received from the church. We had a very strong faith which stood us in good stead. But what people don't understand is that the whole family is handicapped. And it's very important that people understand that, especially the Church. But ministers shy away from the subject: they don't know what to say'.

Those of us who have accepted a member of our family who is mentally handicapped will have learned to love that child, grandchild, brother, sister, cousin. Our feelings may well include regret, impatience, irritation, but underlying that we love them, for themselves, as they are. The genuineness of love has to include what is genuinely there, not just what we imagine or wish to be there.

We must want to share with them as much of our Christian faith as we possibly can. We have no doubt that they are dear to God. It matters that they should know that, if it is humanly possible.

We are grateful when others understand something of this, and also accept and love them within the family of God as they are, not with hideous fears or sentimental notions of what they are imagined to be. Let love be genuine.

FAITH BOWERS

KEEP THEM IN THE COMMUNITY

"Keep them in the community", say all the 'experts'. It is not right to shut the mentally handicapped away in hospitals and to deny them the right of ordinary, everyday life within the community. They have the right to live as normal a life as possible within the limits of their subnormality. So go the arguments and discussions, and it all sounds fine. But what does it mean in practice?

For the more able mentally handicapped children there are some short-term hostels and there are possibilities for long term hostel placement for school leavers. The provision may not yet meet demand but steps are being taken in that direction, and at least some form of short-term care is available on a regular basis. Whilst delighted that this is so, and realizing that in some areas the provision is all too inadequate, my greatest concern is for the most profoundly mentally handicapped children for whom there is almost no provision at all.

Most schools for children with profound learning difficulties have within them units for children with special needs - these are the children, and therefore the families, who have the greatest needs and the least provision to meet those needs.

In the school where I work we have two such Special Needs Units - one for children who have behavioural and other difficulties which prevent them moving through the school in the way the other children do, and one for children who are severely physically, as well as mentally, handicapped. Many of the children in both units are doubly incontinent, several have severe epileptic fits and none of them have any meaningful language. It is hard to imagine what it must be like to have a child who never speaks to you and rarely even looks at you.

There is the sixteen year old boy who is tall and handsome, apart from the wild look in his eye and his erratic, constant movements - waving his hands and stamping his feet continually. He communicates his needs in no uncertain way - dragging an adult to show what he needs, shouting loudly and vigorously while doing so. He must be watched constantly, day and night, as he has no sense of danger and will eat literally anything he finds. These 'finds' have included a large plastic bag, fingers from a rubber glove, and a fourteen inch shoelace.

There is the eleven year old boy who is physically deformed, lies in a wheelchair, unable to support himself, apart from minimal head control. He is doubly incontinent, unable to make eye-contact or express his needs in any way at all. Every day he has at least one or two fits, of varying severity.

Then there is the extremely pretty three year old girl, with bright blue eyes, fair hair and a radiant smile. She has a degenerative disorder of the central nervous system. Already she is almost totally deaf, her eye-sight is rapidly going, she is in more and more pain as nerve endings are affected. The present is grim for her and the future limited, yet she still smiles heart-breakingly on her good days.

And so I could go on. Just over a quarter of the children in the school are in the Special Needs Units, each one with his or her own particular problems and needs which have to be met, each one is loved and cared for at home and is a tremendous credit to their parents and families.

How do families cope with children and situations like these? How are the needs of the handicapped child and the needs of the normal children in the family all met? How do parents cope with their own feelings - most of them feel guilt at having produced a less than perfect child, there is grief at the loss of the normal child they expected to have, they may blame themselves or each other. At best a handicapped child imposes a tremendous strain on any marriage and many marriages do not survive the strain. How do parents cope with the sheer exhaustion of caring for a profoundly mentally handicapped child twenty-four hours a day for life?

For these families there seems to be little or no help. "Keep them in the community" means leave Mum and Dad to cope as best they can. So where can they get the help and support they need?

The greatest need of these families is often to have good friends - someone to listen to them, someone to care about their problems, someone to babysit or take the handicapped child for a while so the other children in the family can have some attention. It is all too easy for parents of mentally handicapped children to become isolated at the time when they most need friends. It is not easy to have baby-sitters if the 'baby' is sixteen years old, hyper-active and extremely difficult to manage, or if the child is likely to have a fit. It is not easy to have visitors or go out to tea if your child is uninhibited and likely to behave in a socially unacceptable way. It is not easy to go out shopping and run the risk of criticism of your child's behaviour.

As parents get older and less able to cope the children become more difficult to cope with, if only because they are bigger and heavier to lift and move around. There is no prospect of them ever leaving home, and there is the added sorrow of parents at losing the prospect of grandchildren. Parents of normal children do not expect to care for their children for life. Why should parents of mentally handicapped children be expected to? And there is always the nightmare question of what happens to the child when parents are unable to cope any more or when they die.

So where does the church come in? What should we be doing to help? Dreams of short-term care and high-dependency hostels will, I believe, come true in time. Units within housing schemes need careful planning and take time to build - we should start working for them now, but it will be too late for many who need help and support immediately. The sheer weight of their problems, plus physical and mental exhaustion, means that many of these families will not be in our church buildings - but Jesus called his disciples to go out and seek; to be good neighbours; to be good friends; to show his love and concern to those in need. That is what we should be doing for these families now.

"Keep them in the community": we are that community, and we must take our share of the responsibility, love and care.

MARLENE FOX

CATHY

(A number of parents have told the Working Group their stories, and their experience underlies the general observations in this book. One example is given here to illustrate what it can be like in more detail.)

Our mentally handicapped daughter Catherine is 'not a type'. She has an I.Q. of about 30, cannot read or write, and has to have help and supervision with all her personal requirements. She was our first child, born three weeks prematurely and, though slow in feeding, there was no apparent sign of handicap. She was a 'bonny baby'. At 17 months, due to her lateness in walking and talking, she was examined by our G.P. who could find nothing wrong. We were told not to worry, she was a normal healthy child.

When she started infant school, there was an evident lack of concentration and she was referred to a child specialist. The results of examination and X-rays showed nothing abormal, and though her IQ was low for her age, we were informed that special education would help. A reasonably bright future was forecast for her.

Two and a half years later we moved, and she had to be re-assessed to decide future education in Bristol. I attended the assessment with her and was concerned, for I felt she was capable of doing better. We were informed that Catherine was incapable of receiving or benefiting from formal education and therefore she would have to attend the junior part of the Bush Training Centre. (Mental handicap training was at that time controlled by Social Services). This letter from the Education Authority came as a shattering blow, but one which had to be accepted.

When we moved to Bristol, Cathy was a very quiet, affectionate, well-behaved child. We could take her anywhere without worry. She has always gone to Church with us – one of the highlights of her week. Basically she is well behaved and sings with feeling the hymns she knows. She loves to greet the people she knows – and doesn't. It is 'Hello' to everyone.

She settled into the training centre very well and for the first three to four years made good progress. Then at twelve years the problems suddenly started and she had periods of regression. She became very hyperactive and her concentration deteriorated. The transfer at sixteen to the adult section was traumatic. From being in a special care group of eight, she was now in a large workshop of 150 – about 30 in her section. After two years she was transferred to a new Training Centre which opened on our side of the city and was very happy there, but in six years never progressed beyond the first special care section.

Behaviour problems increased and she became difficult to handle. From being quiet and well-behaved she became extremely noisy, unpredictable and possessive. Her speech, which had been quite good, deteriorated and she stuttered a lot. She demanded attention and had to be first. If my husband and I started a conversation she would immediately interrupt. She tried to play us off against each other. The same would happen when talking to anyone at Church or outside – a type of jealousy. About this time my mother's health became poor and she needed more attention and so the demands grew.

A medical student used to come and babysit on the rare occasions when Bob and I wished to go out. Previously a very good friend had helped. We did receive more help from people and organisations outside the Church over these difficult years. Cathy started attending a play group run by medical students every Saturday during term time from 11 a.m. to 3 p.m. They were marvellous, arranging varied programmes and outings. She also went to the Townsend Youth Club for two hours on two evenings a week.

She really enjoyed both play group and club, and we appreciated the hours we had to relax.

If a babysitter was unable to come, our son Andrew, then fifteen, would see she went to bed, provided she was ready before we went out. These were rare occasions. We were never far away and on the end of a phone if required. Rightly or wrongly, the whole family life revolved around Cathy - we became very irritable and edgy with each other over silly little things.

Cathy always went on holiday with us, but at the insistence and persuasion of our social worker we had our first real break when she was eighteen (apart from four days when she was sixteen and I had suffered a nervous breakdown). It was a marvellous holiday and whereas previously I had had to concentrate on Cathy, now I was free to enjoy both my husband's and son's company. The following year she accompanied us again but did not really enjoy herself and only wanted to come home. So after this she had her main holiday with the training centre and went to the local hostel whilst we had two weeks break. This way we all enjoyed our holidays.

As she grew older the obvious sorrow and pain of having a handicapped child came home to us. We truly had not really felt it when she was younger. Seeing girls of her age and younger being baptized, having boy friends, doing and enjoying things normal young adults do. One wondered 'if only...'. I know it does not help, but one is only human, and being Christians doesn't prevent these thoughts coming.

We had always thought of caring for her as long as we were able, but when she was fourteen we were made to realise that at some time in the future, sooner rather than later, in fairness to Cathy and ourselves, the break would have to come. We applied to various organisations, but her I.Q. was too low, and grants from Avon were not forthcoming. Our only hope was the local residential hostel, where at nineteen she was staying three weeks in the year, but when twenty-one even they said they could not cope on a permanent basis, such were her behaviour problems and need of personal attention. They were also having problems at the training centre. We were introduced to Yatton Hall, twenty minutes drive from home, under Farleigh Hospital Administration. At first we were not too happy about this (at least I wasn't), but after visiting and seeing all the activities arranged for them, the care shown, not only by the staff but also by the whole village community, her stays there developed on a regular basis and Cathy was happy about it.

After a while we were informed that they would be willing to offer a residential placement to Catherine with a view to training her to fit into a Community Hostel. Though I had always said I would never wish her to go into a Hospital Administrated situation, I realised that this was going to be the only offer we would be made - and Yatton Hall was like a hostel. Our son Andrew was approaching O level studies and the tension in the home was, at times, becoming unbearable. Soon someone would break. So we accepted the 'idea', but even then we had to wait eighteen months for a placement. It was quite an emotional time, for offers were made then withdrawn, but the final offer came, again only two weeks after we had been told that due to cut backs there would definitely be no vacancies for two years. Then a telephone call from the senior consultant, and the offer of a place in two weeks time - three months before Andrew's O levels. It really was a miracle, an answer to many prayers, and we accepted.

Cathy was then twenty-four years old, and she has now been at Yatton Hall for two years. She comes home for Christmas, Bank Holidays and week-ends. She is very happy and we are now convinced we made the right decision, especially as she now has medical problems, having recently had some convulsions. Eventually she should go into a fully staffed, very small community hostel (Yatton is due to close in 1991).

The emotional problem hit me a few months after Cathy went to Yatton. Did we do right? Should I have coped longer? I have wept over her more these last two years than ever, but deep down know that for the family's sake and for Cathy herself, it was right. She is happy, not so dependent on us, in a way making a life of her own. Bob, Andrew and I have begun to live a 'normal' family life.

We have tried to give Cathy all the love and care we have been capable of, perhaps too much attention at times. Our greatest concern has been for her future. We want to know that, wherever she is, she will be loved and cared for and happy. Now we feel she will be.

She is a lovely and loving girl and has taught us a lot. Simple love, patience, tolerance, a simple acceptance of life. We feel we are better equipped to understand and help others in similar circumstances. We just pray that we may be used in this way.

PAT BATTARBEE

BEREAVEMENT AND MENTALLY HANDICAPPED PEOPLE

The King's Fund Bereavement Group was started in 1979 to draw attention to the ordinary and special needs of grieving mentally handicapped people. The Group agreed that the grief of ordinary people was not yet fully recognised and that society still had a long way to go in developing a deeper understanding of grieving. Mentally handicapped people were especially vulnerable and likely to have their grief unconsidered. In March 1981 the group issued the King's Fund leaflet 'The Right to Grieve'. It did not set out to advise on how to help bereaved mentally handicapped people, it merely posed questions about some of the issues. In her discussion paper *Bereavement and Mentally Handicapped People* Maureen Oswin explores some of the questions which were posed in that leaflet. This discussion paper is available from the King's Fund Centre, 126 Albert Street, London NW1 7NF, price 75p, and is warmly recommended. The following extracts are from this paper.

"Everyone's death is unique; even when it is expected it seems to those who mourn as if such a thing has never happened to anyone else before. Those who were close to the dead person feel the loss like a sickness. They may be devastated by their grief, having their sense of irretrievable loss mixed with other unexpected, complicated emotions: guilt, anger, remorse, fear.

> No one ever told me that grief is so like fear, the same fluttering in the stomach, the same restlessness... (C. S. Lewis)

"For a while those who mourn are special people, set apart, requiring respect and sympathy; allowances are made for them, they are expected to need time to adapt to the loss and the changes in life style that it will bring."

"People who are mentally handicapped are sometimes thought of as a collective group who can easily be identified and labelled. it is still common to hear them described as 'childlike', 'dangerous', 'defenceless', 'uncontrollable', 'happy and friendly', 'unable to speak for themselves'. Such stereotyping is unjust. People who have mental handicaps are each very different. Their abilities vary, as do their background experiences, their family life, friends, education, interests, ideas, attitudes and ambitions. Their behaviour will be influenced by their individual experiences. Unfortunately, grieving mentally handicapped people may lack consideration because society continues to have stereotyped ideas about them and consequently may not appreciate that their emotional responses to death and their emotional needs when under stress are the same as the responses and needs of ordinary people."

"It would seem helpful to establish the following principles:

One: There is no reason to think that people who are mentally handicapped will not go through stages of mourning, as do other people.

Two: Mentally handicapped people have as much right as other people to be given consideration when their relatives and friends die.

Three: Each person who is mentally handicapped is an individual and will grieve as an individual; there is no reason to expect them to react in some particular way because they are mentally handicapped.

Four   Some people who are mentally handicapped have particular disabilities so they may need some special help when they become bereaved."

One example tells of Jane, who lived at home with elderly parents and happily attended the local Adult Training Centre. After a long illness, when Jane helped care for him, her father died at home. Jane saw him in the coffin, attended the funeral, and helped prepare the mourners' meal. Mother told her Dad was with Jesus. Jane returned to the ATC, tearfully but bravely. Warmed by her friends' sympathy, she painted pictures about his death, made a pottery vase for the grave, and the drama class acted going to funerals. At home she helped her mother as they both came to terms with their loss. They went out less, without the car. Jane suffered bouts of depression for a few months, but gradually settled to a quiet but secure life.

Two years later Jane's mother saw her off one morning, then had a heart attack and died. That night Jane was whipped off to a hospital twenty miles away. The social worker had collected a case of her clothes, but did not take Jane home for fear it would upset her. Jane was in a strange place where no one knew her, nor understood her signing - a homemade system, which the ATC staff had come to terms with. The distant relative who arranged the funeral had never met her and did not think it appropriate for her to attend. Over the next few weeks secure, peaceful, happy Jane became anxious, quarrelsome, even aggressive. Concerned visitors from the ATC were told they disturbed her, for she wept when they spoke of her mother. Eventually Jane settled into passive and withdrawn behaviour. People were kind and meant well, but they did not seem able to consider her as a person who was mourning.

When offering love and support to anyone within a Christian community there ought to be a greater measure of understanding about the bewildering and conflicting emotions which the bereaved person may be experiencing. It is especially difficult for someone who is mentally handicapped to grasp the significance of the Christian hope of the resurrection. One mentally handicapped lady was reassured to be told that Jesus met the new body of her much loved parent where the old one was left, i.e. at the crematorium.

Like all bereaved people the mentally handicapped will need much reassurance, and many opportunities to go over the events again and again. But what about those people who are unable to talk, and whose understanding is very limited indeed? In her study, Maureen Oswin describes one such lady who, when admitted to hospital after her mother died, refused to eat and the staff feared that she would pine away. "The only comfort she seemed to get was through cuddling. But after a few weeks they discovered that she was most content in the kitchen amongst the smells of cooking and she particularly liked to suck pieces of toast and marmite. They believed that she had probably spent a great deal of time in the kitchen with her mother".

There is no short cut through the bewildering process of grief, and it is recognised that all grieving people need special support and love. This applies equally to all of us, but very special help is needed for men and women who are mentally handicapped.

AUDREY SAUNDERS

THE LOCAL CHURCH AND MENTALLY HANDICAPPED PEOPLE

Notes on a course held at Bristol Baptist College, May 1985

As part of its lay-training programme, Bristol Baptist College organised a pastoral course for lay-people on this topic in May 1985. The object was to help sensitivity and understanding on the part of members with recognised pastoral gifts in their local churches, who could in turn be an important resource for those churches. The course was not advertised publicly, since in the first place the size of the group needed to be limited to a maximum of about twelve, and secondly we wished to recruit only those who, in the opinion of their ministers, would benefit from the course and who, in turn, would be able to help their local churches.

Ten people attended as a result, from Baptist churches in the Bristol area (8 women, 2 men). The sessions were held on four consecutive Thursday evenings, 9-30th May, 7.30-9.00 p.m.

Participants were informed of the purpose of the course as 'to help them increase their understanding of mentally handicapped people, the problems they and their families face, and of how the local church can be welcoming, caring and supportive towards them in the love of Christ'.

The four sessions were as follows:

1. 'Who are the Mentally Handicapped?'
    Mr Leslie Johnson, Chairman of the League of Friends of Purdown Hospital, shared his experiences of befriending and working with mentally handicapped people over the years.

2. 'Christian Understanding and Care'
    The Revd Bryan George and Mrs Faith Bowers, of the Baptist Union Working Group on Mental Handicap and the Church, led an evening on the needs of the handicapped and their families, the problems in counselling etc., with the aid of a video.

3. 'Making Friends'
    This was a visit to Purdown Hospital, arranged by Mr Johnson, to see the social centre provided by the Hospital Friends, and to meet residents and working staff.

4. 'The Family and the Church'
    The concluding evening focussed on the experience of one family in particular, in a Baptist Church in Bristol. Pat and Bob Battarbee told the story of their own mentally handicapped daughter, Catherine and of the ways in which their church

24

had, or had not, been of help to them.

Comments on the course

Those who attended expressed great appreciation for the course. Clearly it met a felt need, among both those who had some experience of the area concerned, and those who at first admitted that they were not even clear as to the difference between mental handicap and mental illness. A factor which lent urgency to the sessions was the present government policy of relocating mentally handicapped people in the community rather than in residential institutions. It was felt that this was a development of which every local church should be made aware. Most local churches are going to come into direct contact with mentally handicapped people more frequently than before.

There is no reason why similar courses of this type should not be set up elsewhere, whether by groups of churches, Associations, Councils of Churches, or whatever. We felt that the smaller size of group was important - there is a need for frank and honest sharing of emotional hang-ups and this can only take place as people get to know one another in the course of an evening and over several weeks. Most local areas would have enough expertise and experience, if looked for, to do something of this sort, especially if backed up by the Baptist Union Working Group. (Members were also supplied with the Church of England booklet on *The Local Church and Mentally Handicapped People*).

In retrospect, I think we could have done with another evening, since we did not really have time to explore the profound theological questions about God's creative purpose, the nature of faith as an *understanding* faith, and so on, which mental handicap prompts.

K. W. CLEMENTS

THE CHURCH IN THE COMMUNITY

Attitudes to mental handicap are changing. The authorities are looking at ways of making better provision and of raising the level of awareness in the community. The church dare not lag behind. It is sobering to realise that the Victorian classifications, 'idiots' and 'imbeciles', lasted as late as 1959. It is even more recent – only since 1970 – that Education Authorities, as well as Health and Social Services, have had responsibility for mentally handicapped children.

Now there are special nurseries and play groups, special schools, youth clubs, adult training centres, sheltered workshops, special sports gatherings. It all sounds – and is – much better. There are still gaps: better provision demands more resources, which are ever scarce.

Advertisements in the newspapers remind us of the constant need for foster and adoptive parents for mentally handicapped children. For adults, too, homes are needed, and many Christian parents see a particular need for homes where their sons and daughters can continue to live in a Christian environment.

Are Christians to be found providing homes, influencing public opinion, staffing schools and clubs, being good neighbours? In this section the changes in provision and consequent needs will be considered. Many Christians are active in these fields. Many churches have not yet begun to think about the mentally handicapped.

Some churches have already responded corporately to the challenge. Various ways they have found to help will be described. The Baptist Union Working Group welcomes news of other such initiatives: it is an area where sharing ideas and experience can inspire and encourage others.

HEALTH SERVICES AND THE MENTALLY HANDICAPPED

Health Services for the mentally handicapped have rightfully been the subject of criticism over a period of many years. In a different generation the public response to the problem of mental handicap was to develop large hospitals or colonies, which often provided a home many miles from the place of origin. The hospitals were self-contained, providing a full 'village life' for the residents. For some residents, usually the more profoundly handicapped, the ideal of a 'village' social life has not been achieved as they have remained daily and yearly on wards without adequate social contact. In addition, old-fashioned dormitory-style buildings have not allowed for the development of privacy and self-esteem.

Problems arising from institutional care of this kind have given rise to numerous enquiries regarding abuses and lack of facilities. These have often overshadowed the many aspects of fine work being carried out. Expectations have changed, and it is often the hospital staff themselves who have been in the forefront of the demand for improvement in conditions. In many cases 40 or 60 bedded wards were the 'norm' until the 1970s. More recently attempts have been made to convert wards into homes of between 12 to 30 residents, with a considerable improvement in personalised facilities and atmosphere. The next step must be to convert these homes into smaller self-contained family units for those who have to remain within the hospital environment or for whom the hospital has been 'home' for such a long time that it would be cruel to move them. Small developments of this kind are already taking place within the hospital setting. Generally financial and staff resources have not been reduced as numbers of residents have reduced, thus allowing for improvement.

Radical change is also arising from national policy that no mentally handicapped children should any further live in hospital. Children in hospital are being moved out into community settings in a programme that should be completed in the very near future. Children who cannot live with their family either for short periods or for longer term care will be cared for in small local community units, either managed by health or social services or by independent organisations.

Local units and facilities are also being developed to enable the discharge of residents from hospitals who can live in small communities or homes. Considerable care has to be taken in the placement of each person in order to ensure an improved quality of life. Social isolation should not be a problem in an enlightened hospital community, but it can be a terrifying consequence of discharge into the community, if dogma is the only reason for change.

Where hospitals for the mentally handicapped remain, they will either provide a home for a smaller number of people requiring long or short term care, or provide specialist facilities for the treatment of the mentally handicapped. Increasing attention has been given over the past years to the development of special skills in the field of mental handicap care. Physiotherapists, Occupational and Speech Therapists, Psychologists, Health Visitors and Nurses, to name but a few of the health service professions, are developing programmes of training and treatment unthought of until recent days. Many will deal with the mentally handicapped and their families in their own homes where the practical problems of daily living can more realistically be tackled. 'Community mental handicap teams' have been developed rapidly over the last ten years and will, in course of time, be seen as the 'front line' in the care and treatment of the mentally handicapped throughout the country. Health service professionals with their colleagues in social services are providing family support as soon as the knowledge of handicap is identified in the young child. In addition to providing treatment and support, the 'team' will also give advice on the range of facilities and relief available. In most areas, booklets are available, detailing the statutory services, voluntary organisations, and support groups relevant to the needs of the handicapped.

It is therefore apparent that there has been a considerable change over recent years in the approach of health services to the care of the mentally handicapped. This is due both to the development of professional expertise and interest, as well as public demand for change. However, as the doors of hospitals close over coming years two major challenges remain. The first of these is to gain public acceptance regarding the place of the mentally handicapped in the community and the second to ensure that those whom we care for are developing a life style that we would welcome for ourselves.

FRANK POWELL

THE TRANSITION TO COMMUNITY CARE

The practice of caring for mentally handicapped people in large
institutions, often remote from urban areas, is a legacy from another
age. But, unlike monetary legacies which often are spent
all-too-soon, this legacy seems to defy all attempts to exhaust it -
and there are several good reasons why this is so.

First, there are still considerable numbers of people cared for
in these hospitals who were committed there as "idiots" or "feeble
minded" during the inter-war years, directly as a result of their
being involved in what, by the standards of today, can only be
called petty criminal acts. Someone then who was slightly mentally
retarded might steal sweets from a shop, break a window or two, or
frighten someone by bizarre behaviour. They soon found themselves
committed to hospital for what has proved to be a very long time.
Such folk were joined by girls who, again often but slightly
retarded, had become pregnant outside marriage. These groups,
inappropriately placed, have lived in hospital now for many decades,
finding companionship and affection in the only home they can
remember. It cannot be compassionate to indiscriminately force these
people out into what we call "the community" but what is to them a
foreign and hostile environment.

Then there are those who, by reason of their degree of
physical or mental handicap, can be justly seen to need "asylum" in
the true sense of the word. There is legitimate questioning as to
whether that asylum needs to be in a large hospital, but there is no
doubt that such an environment has both advantages and
disadvantages. Advantageous is the way in which skilled care can be
made available at all times at high, but still relatively reasonable,
cost compared with that of a small unit. Whereas fairly minimal levels
of hospital care can today cost £11,000 per annum per person,
smallness of scale can easily double that, and it is a harsh fact of
life that this cost has to be met from taxation, that there are still
many who require such care, and that very few of us raise a shout
of acclamation when our taxes, direct or indirect, rise. The
disadvantages of large institutions, in stifling individuality, masking
low standards of care, and in becoming staff-orientated as against
resident-orientated, are well and painfully documented both here and
overseas, and are very difficult to overcome. It is therefore a
welcome step forward that, in the last few years, numerous domestic
scale care units have been developed around the country, and are
now successfully providing homes for many more severely
handicapped people.

The transition from hospital to community-based care can be a
very lengthy one now that most of those making this journey are in

the categories of those with marked handicaps, physical and mental. Severe deficits of the sensory system, profound physical handicap, intractable epilepsy, or bizarre and seriously disturbed behaviour patterns characterise many of these people. Their training and habilitation is only achieved over periods of time measured in many months or even years, using personalised, detailed, and constantly updated therapy and training programmes based on continuing assessment and, where it is practicable, detailed measurements and ratings. Some of this work is carried out at ward level, some in special training units. Progress is carefully noted and rewarded, and may well commence in areas such as day and night continence, feeding skills, dressing and grooming, simple motor skills, basic sounds or speech, or in inter-personal contact with other residents or with staff. Later stages may reach areas such as counting, recognition of money, simple tasks around the ward, writing the name, or recognising objects by name, in preparation for a gentle and gradual introduction to the complex world beyond.

When a handicapped person begins to reach the stage where movement into a more natural environment becomes a real possibility, great care is taken to see that the proposed surroundings appear to be compatible with their individual needs, or can be made so, and with the creation of a socially, emotionally, and temperamentally complementary group to make up the new family, for that is what is in fact being created. It is a family unit whose members have to learn to live in close proximity to each other - and we know how difficult that can be for a 'real' family! The members of the families being created in this way have, if anything, a much greater need for mutual help and support than the average household.

My own experience in this field has been in the last year or two in the acquisition, adaptation and provision of a four-bedroomed house two hundred yards from the hospital entrance, for use by four moderately handicapped people, two of each sex, of mixed ages. The transformation which has taken place in each of the four over the many months during which their training has been painstakingly progressed by dedicated staff, has been incredibly great and incredibly rewarding to watch. The climax came only last week when they felt confident enough to invite all those who had helped them to afternoon tea at the house, and we experienced the warmth of human feeling of that newly created family unit, so different as individuals, yet so very much sharers in a wonderful, new and for so long unimagined experienced. No - unfortunately it is almost impossible to get a newspaper to print such news, although they are always willing to headline the reaction of neighbours when one proposes to establish such a unit and the loud cries of protest, indignation, and fear borne of ignorance resound across the rooftops.

It is, for such a group, at this time when a welcoming

individual or group can make such a difference with the gift of true and selfless friendship, devoid of patronising or condescending spirit. Perhaps one of the most important skills to be brought to such a relationship will be the need to discern the borderline between help which renders the recipient less able to help himself and more dependant, and help which promotes independence and self-help. Patience is certainly a necessary grace at all times. The prospect of a welcome into another discrete social group such as a church fellowship, or a club, could also assist tremendously at this time, enabling the handicapped person to assimilate progressively into 'normal' society and to mix with others apart from their previously limited contacts.

If you feel that, either as an individual or as one of a group, you could help in this way there are several approaches which you could use. One would be to write either to the Administrator or to the Director of Nursing Services at the hospital nearest to your home. Details will be readily found at your local Reference Library in the *Hospital and Health Services Year Book*. The index to this annual publication is at the back of the book, on green paper, and you will find hospitals listed both by name and by the speciality involved. You could, alternatively, make contact through your local Community Health Council, whose Secretary's name and address are usually to be found posted on a notice board at the Library. Or you may get in touch through the Hospital League of Friends or through the Hospital Voluntary Services Coordinator.

Such a home may be fully staffed, or it may be intermittently visited either by hospital or by Community Nursing staff. If operated by Social Services, contact would need to be through their local Area Office. It may be known as a 'Group Home', and it is well to distinguish this kind of provision from what is most usually known as a Community Mental Handicap Unit (although the name does vary across the country) which is larger, fully staffed, and where therefore the opportunity and need for voluntary effort is generally less and of a different nature. Such a unit will normally accommodate more severely handicapped people, often with a high proportion of short stay and respite care.

Before you put pen to paper, or pick up the telephone to offer your help, a word of warning. Do not contemplate becoming involved unless you are quite certain that you and anyone with you have the staying power required. So many well-intentioned people launch into such a project, only to sink without trace within weeks. The reasons are often entirely justifiable, but the effect of such discontinuity on those you seek to help can be disastrous. To become involved in such a project is no small thing, since real lives, feelings, and personalities are bound up in its success or failure. The rewards, however, are correspondingly great.

BRIAN WINDSOR

NEIGHBOURS TO PEOPLE WITH HANDICAP

Most of the ladies and gentlemen now being moved to small houses in the community will have little or no say in where they live. They will be moving from what must seem to many to be a 'safe community' to an unknown one. Unless they are accepted and made welcome, they may become very isolated and lonely. That is why the Hospital Chaplaincy in Oxfordshire recently arranged a day conference, through the Oxford diocesan committee, to discuss ways in which those in the churches can be good neighbours to people with a mental handicap.

When people live in a hospital, there is a hospital chaplain. The idea of a community chaplain is new. In Oxfordshire it has now been established that a community chaplaincy is necessary to the multidisciplinary team responsible for the change from hospital to community. Eventually there will be a chaplains for group homes in each district, appointed from within the local community. This is regarded as a forerunner for what could become general policy. The first such chaplaincies, with Church of England, Roman Catholic and Free Church members, have already been set up.

The Community Chaplains will have a responsibility to support the residents, staff, and relatives, and to enable the local community, especially the churches, to play their proper role as good neighbours. They will not have the direct pastoral care of the residents, which rightly falls to the local clergy, but they will be advocates for the residents to ensure that they have the resources and support for spiritual growth and choice.

Mentally handicapped men and women, like the rest of us, need to be welcomed individually, not just en masse. They do not all enjoy the same activities, and they do not always want to go out together in a group. They need to be accepted as people in their own right. In doing this, we allow them to make their own contribution to the local community. True friendship has to be reciprocal, and many mentally handicapped men and women have much to offer.

Some are more dependent and need constant care. The people providing this care, be they parents or professionals, also need to be accepted and supported.

Some houses or flats with more able residents may have very little professional support. Although every mentally handicapped person is entitled to help from a social worker, the amount of help given varies widely from one area to another. Our handicapped neighbours may need help from us, both to ensure that they are receiving all available professional help and to fill the gaps. A letter from the DHSS advising a change in benefit, with an appropriate form enclosed for completion, can cause great anxiety to people whose reading ability is limited or nil!

If you are good at filling in forms; if you have gardening skills which you could pass on; if you are a member of a local social or sporting club, then you you have much to offer your new neighbours. If you can also offer the opportunity to share in worship, and experience the presence and peace of God, then you will be a friend indeed.

AUDREY SAUNDERS

THE NEW NEIGHBOURS

Greenwich Health Authority opened Arnold House, a hostel for mentally handicapped adults, in November 1984. The site, built around the shell of an old cottage hospital, is on the busy A207, and almost exactly opposite Blackheath and Charlton Baptist Church.

The thirty-two residents had previously lived in Darenth Park Hospital, amid the green fields of north Kent. Some of them have been in institutions for thirty or forty years, and some were not placed there because they were mentally handicapped but for social reasons, such as having an illegitimate baby or being orphaned and of slightly below normal intelligence.

In the recent past, Blackheath and Charlton Baptist Church members had mourned the death of Margaret Towy-Evans, who had kept house for her sister, now church secretary, for fifteen years, and who had herself been mentally handicapped. Her love and often extremely apt, insightful or witty comments are sadly missed. Through Margaret, members had begun to learn a little about caring for mentally handicapped people.

More recently Brenda had been attending the church. Brenda lives in another local authority hostel. She has a delight in birthdays unsurpassed among adults in my experience, and was radiant with joy when the congregation sang "Happy Birthday, Brenda" on her 37th birthday which fell on a Sunday.

But how were we to cope with the sudden influx of eight or ten different mentally handicapped people who began attending the services soon after their arrival at Arnold House? Some were easily accepted. Quiet Tom slips in with no fuss. George came, and delighted some with his pride in his new suit. But what about Frank? Younger than most of the Arnold House residents, and with a collection of Roman Catholic religious pictures and statuettes, he was more difficult to ignore. He sings loudly and to his own high pitched tunes during the hymns and songs. The drugs he takes cause some uncontrollable shaking in his hands at times, and he talks very rapidly, so that it can be hard to understand what he says. Frank keenly wants to be accepted, and has offered to clean the church.

On the whole these were the minor problems. More difficult are the unexpected spin-offs of long institutionalisation on these near neighbours of ours. Maud was used to sitting at the front at the chapel services at Darenth Park. So attending morning service at Blackheath and Charlton she made her way, on her walker, to the very front row. On the day of the Sunday School Anniversary this paid off handsomely as she, sitting among the younger children, was offered and accepted the choice of a sweet from one of two bags! But on another occasion a deacon leading singing with his guitar was chatting about how parents check up on their children: "Have you cleaned your teeth? Washed your hands?", Whereupon Maud decided her hands needed washing at that moment and made a noisy exit from the service, and re-entrance ten minutes later.

We soon learned that Ron, who talked non-stop for three days when he arrived at Arnold House, would need to have a special eye kept on him. One church member has an informal liaison role between the hostel staff and the church and this has proved very helpful. Ron's persistent chatter through prayers and the sermon were discussed with the care assistants, and then with Ron himself.

Several Arnold House residents came to a church Bank Holiday family evening of food, slides and silly games. Soon an invitation came to the church and about thirty of us went to Sunday tea at Arnold House. Among the group were some of our young men who were surprised how much they enjoyed themselves. One or two older church ladies who had come with very mixed feelings found it much easier to talk to their new friends in their own surroundings, and it was a very happy and successful occasion.

But what is the answer to Frank's constant question as he eyes the church bookstall: "Have you got any books for me?"

TRISHA DALE

34

THE HOSPITAL CHAPLAIN

A number of ministers serve as part-time chaplains to subnormality hospitals. More may well be asked to engage in such work with the new community homes. Many will find it a daunting prospect - and not all would have the appropriate patience and skills. As with all work with the mentally handicapped, it is 'not the sort of work you can put someone in just because it has to be done'. The local minister may not always be the best person to care for the local home. Some, however, who are not instinctively attracted to such work, may prove good at it.

John Stroud, of South Street Baptist Church in Exeter, is Free Church Chaplain to a local hospital. When he started in this work he was not prepared for the spontaneity of the mentally handicapped. He was taken aback by their cuddles, and at first found he retreated into himself. It took time to adjust and learn to delight in their uninhibited greetings. Since then he has seen others alarmed at their first exposure to the mentally handicapped. Sometimes patients are aggressive, but that too may appear worse than it really is - they have so few means of communication.

John tries to visit four units with twenty residents once a fortnight. He is known as 'the man from the church', and has learned he does not have to convey anything verbal. If he can convey acceptance, warmth and hope, that conveys something of the Christian faith. It may just be by holding hands for a while. He thinks this one-to-one pastoral contact is more important than the monthly service in the Occupational Therapy department. That is difficult because of the ability range - from those of 12 year old mental age through to those who can respond but not communicate.

The chaplain also works with the staff, and here the role is different. Rapid changes in the care of the mentally handicapped are making a 'Cinderella' service far more professional, and it is not easy for some to adjust to the new approaches. At a recent training week, John was invited to talk about the chaplain's role, a welcome recognition of his part in the team. He comments that how much the chaplain can do depends partly on staff help, and staff are more willing to co-operate if the patients enjoy the chaplain's activities.

Lloyd Ozanne, a full-time hospital chaplain in Sheffield, observes that 'most ministers find ministry to the mentally handicapped frustrating because they are used to conceptualise their teaching so are at a loss to communicate with the disabled in thought capacity. The gifted in teaching young children are much more successful'.

He divides the handicapped into three main categories.

- The severely handicapped, without any capacity to conceptualise, in need of total care. 'There is little the Church can offer to them other than a very practical offer to support the carers and relatives'.

- The moderately handicapped, who have varying capacity of understanding. 'They enjoy sharing with others in activity, therefore will like to share in worship'. Music, objects, pictures, drama, are all helpful in communicating with them.

- Persons with a capacity for learning and remembering, who may simply need a guiding hand in running their lives. 'If members of churches can overcome their fear and shyness to give them a welcome, they can easily be absorbed into the family which is the Church'. They 'can assimilate teaching well presented. The sacraments of Baptism and Holy Communion are particularly meaningful to them... Their capacity to love and be loved is often a true reflection of that love which is the hallmark of Christianity'.

From Birmingham Edwin Newton writes of his 'retirement job' as part-time Free Church Chaplain at Monyhull Hospital. In addition to Sunday worship, they hold a 'Church Evening' on Tuesdays, with much singing and simple instruction. A lending library of colourful magazines is enjoyed. A few friends come in from local churches to help, especially by playing the organ and pushing wheelchairs to the chapel.

Churches may back up their minister's work as chaplain. At New North Road, Huddersfield a Carol Service has been conducted in the local hospital for some eighteen years. Knowing that regular repetition is urged in work with the mentally handicapped, we queried whether once a year was enough to be remembered. Mrs Valerie Green wrote back, 'Yes, we are remembered, along with what we sing. The carols are very popular... they like the happy tunes they can clap along with... The patients like to hug and kiss us afterwards, and enjoy a chat. The prayer and short talk is enjoyed - it is the simple Christian message in the simplest way, but well received, because we are fresh faces to them'. There is pathos in Mrs Green's final remark: 'We often leave them photos of our children, which they ask for'. So little *can* mean so much.

HOW CHURCHES ARE HELPING

Although long-term homes are available for mentally handicapped adults, relatively few are run as Christian homes. As one mother writes, 'There must be many, many handicapped children in our denomination alone whose parents have the same yearning to provide some Christian follow-up for them when they are no longer able to cope with or care for them. This is the largest problem parents have for their children'. That widowed mother has been so 'burdened about the provision of a Christian home' that even while seeking a long-term home her daughter could go to later, she has herself fostered a younger boy with similar handicap.

Several Baptist churches have been involved in setting up Christian homes, often in conjunction with housing charities, such as Christian Concern for the Mentally Handicapped, Guideposts Trust, and the Shaftesbury Society. Peter Bowes, minister of Morningside Baptist Church in Edinburgh, has described how a mentally handicapped woman, homeless after her mother died, pestered the church to help her - 'You're Christians. DO something!' A group from the church began to look into the matter. They were encouraged by the work of L'Arche, and in 1977 set up the Ark Housing Association Ltd. Within seven years Ark had ten houses in Scotland, with 100 residents, and more planned.

There are quite a number of Christian homes now - but not enough. People may have to go a long way to find one. Loving parents, as they grow older, would naturally like to settle their son or daughter within reach, where they can keep in touch.

Where the mentally handicapped grow up within the church family, churches usually try to make them welcome. Many a Sunday School, Brownie Pack, Boys Brigade, or youth club has one or more educationally subnormal members. One Hampshire church reports its own special, single story, Scripture examination, with coaching and certificate, for a girl with Down's Syndrome, 'making her feel the same as the rest'.

Some churches have gone further, seeking out the mentally handicapped of their neighbourhood.

The Children's Centre of West Ham Central Mission has for eleven years run an Opportunity Group for all handicapped under-fives, with their mothers and brothers and sisters. The work is supported by local Social Services, including some help from speech and physiotherapists. It aims to provide good play opportunities, to break down barriers about handicap, to encourage normal children to mix and communicate with the handicapped, and to support the parents. 'The Mums are glad to bring their child into a group where he will be welcomed without judgment, and where he is lovingly handled and encouraged to enjoy himself'. The mothers themselves spontaneously form a close and supportive group, 'they are good at listening'. The leader, Judith Marchant, observes that helping there is 'not everyone's scene – it is hurtful to get alongside the Mums and share their anxiety and hurt'. 'One clear factor does emerge: the best volunteers are practising Christians'.

South Street Baptist Church, Exeter, has a midweek coffee shop, mainly patronised by young mothers, the elderly and the unemployed. Into this five or six children from a special school come for coffee as part of their training. It is a non-threatening context, where they can practise social skills without distress if it goes wrong, a stage between school and a public café.

Westcliff Baptist Church, Essex, runs a Temporary Employment Scheme, with funds from Manpower Services Commission. Amongst their activities is a two-way relationship with the Avro Adult Training Centre. 'Each week for a few hours trainees from Avro come along to our centre as part of their social skills activities. Six help in our canteen – preparing food, washing up, etc. with great enthusiasm. One helps with gardening jobs for the elderly'. Meanwhile several of the Westcliff employees, on MSC grants, work at Avro, and others in local special schools. The Avro Manager reports that the Westcliff workers are valued as 'they offer a different outlook to a member of staff, e.g. a volunteer is not looked upon as superior by the mentally handicapped people'. The volunteers seem more approachable, and that can help draw the handicapped out. Some have built up real friendships which extend beyond working hours.

Stirling Baptist Church, Morningside, Edinburgh, and Haven Green in London run special Bible classes. Two are described later in this book. Morningside has held a fortnightly class for three years, for five or six adults. The leader is a teacher of children with special needs. Activities are similar to those at Stirling. They keep a small library of Bible stories (mainly those published by Lion, and the National Bible Society of Scotland).

At Elm Park in Essex the church runs a holiday club for mentally handicapped children and young people, twice a week, 10 a.m. to 3 p.m. The idea came from a local health visitor, who belongs to the Salvation Army. Minibus transport is provided by the South Essex Mentally Handicapped Association and the local Roman Catholic church. Twenty children attend. The club is staffed by twenty volunteers, plus others in the kitchen. These are drawn from the church, together with other local friends and seniors from the comprehensive school. For those too severely handicapped for this club, members of the church and congregation also run a transport service every week day in the holidays to the neighbouring borough's handicap centre. This work is part of the church's extensive neighbourhood scheme.

Woodgrange Baptist Church, Ilford, recently opened a youth club for the mentally handicapped. Two dozen 14-21 year olds gather on Monday evenings, 5 to 7.30 p.m., and on Fridays a similar number of 8-14 year olds. Some come from private homes, others from special schools. Minibus transport is arranged. This is the only club of its kind in New Ham and 'it doesn't cover the need'. The work is directed by the warden's wife, a qualified teacher of the mentally handicapped, with about six voluntary helpers each evening. Some able youngsters help. 'All the normal facilities are available: table tennis, snooker, craftwork, badminton, hockey, football. Later in the evening the same equipment is used by the 'normal' youth club.

In 1969 the Baptists of Hall Green, Birmingham, began a mentally handicapped youth club. There are now 43 members, aged 16 to 40 - for none have outgrown it! This club meets monthly for two hours on Wednesday evenings. Local Methodists provide the transport. There is no charge: the cost is covered by voluntary effort, supplemented by the church. Most members live with parents, though a few come from a local residential home. Activities include table tennis, 'table games' like dominos and blow football, and dancing. A light supper is enjoyed. The organisation is informal. Usually about eight helpers will be around. The members love people who will sit down and talk to them. As the club has become known locally, various local organisations have been pleased to provide occasional outings.

Baxter Gate, Loughborough, also runs a club. This is slightly different. Known as 'Link Up', it brings handicapped and able together one Saturday evening a month, promoting friendship and co-operation. At other times the handicapped contacts are encouraged to join in the church's other activities. The club's programme includes discos, barn dances, board games, barbecues, six-a-side football, and music. One evening there was a visiting orchestra, with percussion for all. Parents are given a short break, and as the church gradually gets to know them there is increased work in pastoral support.

Elsewhere churches have thrown their efforts in with Mencap, providing premises and help for local Gateway Clubs. The Revd T. Aneurin Davies writes from Anglesey that 'The officers and the majority of the supporters of these clubs are church leaders and prominent church members. Indeed, it can be claimed that the churches are the main supporters of the work done in Anglesey'. The handicapped clubs often contribute an item to services at the church festivals. These are now readily received, 'where once people would have turned away'. The organisers of these clubs report that outings are popular, especially if tea is included! Repeatedly this theme recurs in work with the handicapped: the refreshments, especially where home baking is provided by church members, are a highlight.

A team of church members from Leavesden Road, Watford, visit a ward at the local hospital each week. The church at Ash Street, Bootle, supports a small group home for four adults, two of whom regularly attend services, Christian Endeavour, and social activities. The pastor explains: 'We seek to treat them as the adults that they are... Our mentally handicapped friends not only fit in but rather become an integral part of the fellowship'.

Pear Tree Road, Derby, is an inner-city, multi-racial church, with 'very few members available in the daytime to organise the kind of service to mentally handicapped some churches are able to do', yet for over thirty years they have found ways of caring. Two former ministers were hospital chaplains, and the church supported them, visiting the first hospital and arranging cricket matches and carol concerts, and welcoming a group from the second to Sunday tea and evening worship once a month. Later two members were wardens of a local hostel. Again links were forged. Several of these handicapped adults worship regularly at Pear Tree Road. The church was a bit surprised that a visitor should be struck by this, for 'they are just part of the worshipping community'. One is a baptised member. He cannot read the hymn book, but he can hand them out each Sunday. He and his brother delight in church outings. This church sees its role 'as an accepting and welcoming community where they feel that they belong', and clearly accepts the extra responsibilities this entails as a matter of course.

Two years ago the Baptists of Battle, East Sussex, were asked to house the Battle Day Care Group twice a week. This is a secular organisation, the leader not a Christian, but use of the premises led to church members volunteering to help, and one serves on the committee. The club's activities are described as 'reading, cutting, writing, swimming, typing, use of simple tools'. The minister, Dennis Nolan, welcomed this as helping the church 'to be seen as a caring community in a small town'. In practice it goes beyond that. The contact is bringing new faces into the congregation, and Mr Nolan has been asked to lead occasional services with the group, anniversary thanksgiving and a Christmas carol service. When he wrote he was about to introduce some simple Bible study.

Sometimes seemingly small things can make all the difference. After a relative's death, a mentally handicapped man was able to live on in the family home, with a friend for company. The arrangement was that they attended a Day Centre during the week, and on Sundays the local church took over. Several families undertook to take turns to invite them back after morning worship. Their care extended beyond providing lunch to help with such awkward tasks as washing hair and cutting toe nails. It is lawful to do good on the sabbath!

In her booklet, *Croydon Hall, House of Joy* (2nd part, 1982), Margaret Davies, who was head of a boarding school for educationally subnormal girls near Bristol, told how each year the Broadmead Church asked for a list of three things each pupil would like for Christmas. The list went up at church for people to select items as personal gifts. A new girl, hearing of this, told another, nicknamed Spiky, 'I know, I've been in places where they gives out things'. 'No, you don't then,' said Spiky. 'It's not like that. Your presents have your name on them and they are all sent by good friends'. 'They can't send anything to me. They don't know me'. 'Yes, they will'. 'How could they? Who tells them to do it?' For a moment Spiky hesitated. 'I don't rightly know,' she said, 'but I reckon it's the Lord Jesus Christ'.

A SCOUTING VENTURE

The fifth Carshalton Scout Group is sponsored by Carshalton Beeches Baptist Free Church. In common with many scout groups it consists of Beavers, Cubs, Scouts and Venture Scouts – but there the similarity ends, for it contains *two* Venture units. The second unit is mixed and meets at Orchard Hill, Queen Mary's Hospital. It is small and there are almost as many leaders as scouts because all the members are severely mentally handicapped young people, with a variety of physical and communication disabilities requiring one-to-one attention.

The Scout Movement has welcomed handicapped members for years, normally integrated into able-bodied units and occasionally in special units. There has always been one minimum requirement – that the boy or girl can prove their ability to know and understand the Scout Law and Promise. The communication problems of the Queen Mary's Ventures make this impossible, but the Scout Movement has agreed to view the unit as experimental, with the hope that if it is successful other units will follow. The Scout Movement aims to promote the mental, physical and spiritual growth of all its members, which leaves the Christian leader free to make their own interpretation! The church has an important supporting role for the unit – the most important thing, to the leaders as well as the scouts, is to know that we are loved and accepted. We do not attend church-parade every month (although some leaders accompany our ventures to the hospital chapel service each week), but when we do, our members want to greet as many folk as they can, verbally or a handshake or hug and dribbly kiss. We are very grateful that church folk are so willing to return those greetings and to chat to and assist our young people. This helps the church in its other vital supporting role, that of prayer. It helps in that our ventures become real people to them, not just names, and folk can often rejoice with us in small victories and improvements which they can see for themselves. Occasionally the ventures have helped to lead worship, a moving experience for everyone because of their innocent simplicity.

Our scouting is on a very basic level, with programmes often of a pre-school type content. The weekly meetings of the unit nearly always include the Lord's Prayer, which those who can speak knew and loved before they became scouts, as they also know various children's hymns and choruses which we include too. When we sing, we use percussion instruments, and sign language which all are learning. Simple prayers are sometimes used, particularly for needs such as illness, and we thank the Lord when he answers. Somehow it does not seem to matter what IQ a severely mentally handicapped person has; we believe that although the mind may be retarded, *the spirit is not,* and the Lord seems to meet these beautiful people in his own way. I have noticed a positive response to the name of Jesus, and that he loves an individual by name, even in a youngster whose only communication is by eye (or teeth!).

Small children cannot grasp abstract concepts - neither can our ventures, so everything needs to be put over in concrete terms and with much repetition and may take years to sink in. This may mean that for some, initially prayer only means putting down the jigsaw and folding hands with 'help' while people say meaningless words; but it is a start - that fact of leaving a cherished activity for a period of stillness can be a big step towards understanding reverence for God. *Love* is the one concept which they do seem to grasp and offer unreservedly, so we can learn from them and in returning it can begin to show God's love for them. Rejection by the general public is very painful and leaders have at times been heartbroken by a refusal to reply to a venture's bellowed 'Hello' and the look of bewilderment on his face.

The various parts of the Scout Promise - doing one's best to do duty to God and the Queen, helping other people and obeying the Scout Law, have had to be simplified to a minimum. DUTY TO GOD = prayer, praise, church parade and chapel (all dearly loved). DUTY TO THE QUEEN = keeping the law = 'I must not steal food or bite people' - the ventures all know that these activities lead to punishment, so are wrong, which is the first step towards recognition of sin. HELPING OTHER PEOPLE = picking up something off the floor when asked; pushing a wheelchair safely; making the tea and pouring out cups for other people first – which may require superhuman physical strength on the part of the leaders.

The Scout Law requires qualities somewhat akin to the fruits of the Spirit and takes a little longer ... At present it is hopefully 'caught' from the leaders, whose lives need to be worthy of imitation (back to prayer again!).

We do not claim to have any answers, we are all novices at this work, but we do know that the severely mentally handicapped person has one great advantage over the 'normal' person whose intellect may block faith – the quality of unquestioning acceptance, which, allied with love, can open the door to Christ.

JUDY MARTIN

BOUND TOGETHER IN LOVE

Moving to Gloucestershire in 1972, we came to rest at the United Reformed Church in Painswick. There one of the first families to welcome us were the grandparents of a mentally handicapped girl of nine, and as we had a mentally handicapped daughter aged eight, with three elder brothers, we were immediately involved in both church and local Mencap activities.

Nicola's mother was already on the local Mencap committee and I joined her there, beginning a friendship that lasted until her early death ten years later. I had been involved in our local Spastic Society in Hertfordshire and here in Painswick our joint efforts with church and the Society became intertwined.

Our church has always been most supportive in our welfare and in local fund-raising efforts. Over the years the two have become almost indivisible.

A garden supper held in the village, sometimes with visiting choir or singers, and lots of chat and laughter, became a regular event each year during Mencap Week. So much part of church life and support did it become that its announcement in church notices and the attendance of many members of the congregation was an accepted thing.

There followed an annual Fayre in aid of Mencap held in Stroud every November. Again we have received enormous support from the church. Over the years members have given us gifts in kind and cash, and made the effort to travel into town to the Fayre. Gradually the church has taken on responsibility for the kitchen arrangements. Two church members now organise the meals and helpers: they shop, transport goods and staff, cook and serve hot meals and snacks from 9 a.m. till 5 p.m. At the end of a long day we go downstairs and find the kitchen empty and spotless. The whole event is a huge effort of organisation and hard work. It is, of course, an excellent moneyspinner.

The village, through the churches, also provides the hands necessary for that least attractive of chores - rattling tins, knocking on doors, and delivering envelopes.

Another 'annual' is the Flower Festival, held each year in our church (where the Baptists joined us eighteen months ago to become one non-conformist congregation, Christchurch). The festival was initiated by the URC minister some ten years ago. It is a village effort and draws visitors from far and wide to see the flowers and enjoy coffee, lunch or tea in the church hall or outside. One third of the proceeds always goes to Mencap, the balance to two other charities which vary from year to year.

Last, but by no means least, there is a service in church in Mencap week. This is held in the evening and attended by some mentally handicapped people, some parents and friends, and church members. The aim is to have mentally handicapped people join in as much as possible, so the address is simple and short. This year the young people acted a short sketch to illustrate the reading. The hymns and choruses are well-known, often helped by a singer or guitar, and the Gateway Club usually sing an item on their own. The collection goes to local Mencap. The service is followed by refreshments in the hall, again supplied by church members. It is a delight to see the guests relish the home baking.

The village itself is well used to having mentally handicapped people in its midst. We have had a home for fairly able mentally handicapped adults here for many years and the residents are a familiar sight as they make small purchases in the village shops, have a cup of tea in the local tea-rooms, or attend the parish church. There are also half-a-dozen youngsters living at home, and, two miles away, a Rudolph Steiner training centre for 16-18 year olds.

Perhaps we are unusual in being able to absorb so much handicap within a community of approximately 3500 people, but it is accepted. The continual involvement and support of our church must surely play more than a little part in this.

MARION SADLER

A MATTER OF THEOLOGICAL INTEGRITY

When we look at whether the mentally handicapped are or should be admitted to the sacraments and to church membership, the generosity of response has surprised the Working Group. Far more ministers than expected tell us they are happy to baptise mentally handicapped candidates, and churches welcome them into membership. Christians feel they should respond to the handicapped with kindness, and many find it not too difficult to 'make allowances'. Naturally churches which have taken this course are more likely to volunteer their experience. The Working Group has been aware that there are dissentient murmurs around, but unfortunately they are not easy to catch. We need to listen to those who, not lacking goodwill to the subnormal, feel unable to open _all_ the doors of the church to them. Perhaps it is only parents, their love and concern for a mentally handicapped child beyond question, who can openly express this. There must be others who share their reservations.

Whether a mentally handicapped man or woman should be baptised as a believer, should be accepted for church membership, or should receive communion (with or without these usual precursors), is a matter for the church to decide. There can be no hard and fast rules, because mentally handicapped people differ so much in their understanding and must be considered individually. It should not be left to the parents' judgment alone. It is cheering to find that often these decisions have been carefully made by the church meeting, acting properly according to Baptist understanding.

In the ensuing pages this sensitive area is explored. The questions are recognised, the answers differ, and no-one finds them clear-cut and easy. The last paper in this section is written from a wider experience of severe mental handicap and also from a different theological tradition, which may be refreshing as we seek to evaluate the Baptist position.

INCLUDE THEM OUT?

I am asked whether mentally handicapped people should be baptised and admitted to church membership and the Lord's Supper. Let me assume that when we talk about baptism, church membership and the Supper we are talking about three aspects of the same thing: baptism is the door of the church and the Lord's Supper is the meal of the church. The question then becomes: should mentally handicapped people join the church?

My reply should be prefaced by a warning and one or two explanatory remarks. The warning is that my reply does not amount to an answer. I am in two minds, as my title suggests, and think it better to make that apparent than pretend I have resolved what is for me, as for many, a difficult issue.

One point of clarity which explains and also aggravates my difficulties is that the church cannot be equated either with the Kingdom of God or with the realm of salvation. Being a church member is essentially about being a disciple. It is not about entering the Kingdom or being saved. It certainly has nothing to do with whether God loves us or not. Outside the church, as inside, we are all without doubt the objects of God's love; we may or may not be of the Kingdom; and we shall be more and less saved as the case may be. Church membership makes no decisive difference. What is different is that we have declared, and others have recognised, our intention to be disciples and to follow Christ. This present discussion is not then about whether mentally handicapped people are loved by God, or belong to God's kingdom, or enjoy a measure of salvation. They are and they do. The discussion is about whether they can be disciples.

I should further explain that in agreeing to discuss, however briefly, some of the theological questions raised for the church by mental handicap, I do not agree, and I'm sure no-one else agrees, that they are the most important theological questions. In fact like most of the debates about ordering the church, I find them comparatively unimportant, to be dealt with patiently in an effort to prevent them getting in our way. The more important questions raised by mental handicap have of course to do with evil and a God of love, with what we have to receive rather than give, and with challenges to our over confident views on what it means to be normal human beings. We think we now recognise sexism and racism, even ageism. We have yet to learn to affirm that all who are handicapped are able and all who are able are handicapped.

Finally by way of introduction, the epilogue to my remarks is as important, more so, than this prologue, referring as it does to what, or rather who, makes these questions of immediate interest to me.

What then do we look for in suitable candidates for church membership, without denying that far more is given to them than is expected of them? The traditional answer of most churches would be: confession of sin; a change of heart; faith in the saving work of Christ; commitment to Jesus as Lord; a vocation to Christian witness and service; signs of growing up into Christ; all of which implies understanding and a sense of personal responsibility. All these are required in some measure, if not in equal measure.

The special question posed by mentally handicapped people is what happens to those who are incapable of these responses to the Gospel, always assuming there is some reasonably satisfactory way of assessing their capabilities?

There are some incapable of any response whatsoever, for whom church membership could mean nothing. For others, should we accept a level of response compatible with their capabilities? We cannot wait, as with children, until they are 'ready' since we do not know what progress they will make, and they may never be more ready than they are now. We look then for understanding and responsibility but only of a kind we judge to be within their powers. If they know who Jesus is and love him and want to be with his people, we may judge that to be sufficient. If they are capable of a sense of sorrow for wrongdoing, and if they want to help people as Jesus did, so much the better. They, like everyone else, can only be asked to respond as the people they are. The response may be minimal. It may also be fitful, only capable of being sustained if the handicapped are supported even more than we support more able Christians; but if it is compatible with what we know of them as persons then it is enough.

What I have so far outlined seems to me to be the strictest view our churches should take of the matter; strict in the sense of more likely to exclude handicapped people, not necessarily in the sense of being correct. Perhaps we could say it indicates the most demanding attitude we should take, or a standard below which we should not fall. The following five considerations tend towards a less strict, less demanding or more inclusive view.

1. It is true that we look for a response to the Gospel in those who come to join the church, but we are made members of Christ more by what we are given than by how we respond. As we said, far more is given than is expected. This is the strong point about infant baptism. It stresses that children of Christian families have the faith that follows Christ as a gift, not as the result of any conscious act of their own. When we worry whether handicapped

people have the ability to respond we should not overlook the possibility that, by belonging to a Christian family and already enjoying the company of the Church, they have already received the gift of faith. Do we exclude them because they may not be capable of other responses that certainly matter, but matter less, when they have what matters most; especially where, by definition, we can't have everything?

2.   No single view of the church is adequate, including the view we have implied. The New Testament draws on a wealth of imagery to describe it. Christian history has defined it in many different ways. We must beware of being over cautious about admitting mentally handicapped people to membership because we are narrow minded about the church. They may have difficulty in finding their place in a highly committed intentional band of disciples; but what of them as members of the Body of Christ (maybe nearer the heart and the hand than the head), or of the poor of the earth in whom Christ is especially found, or as those who far from being 'against us' are 'for us', to mention only three examples?

3.   So far we have tied the Lord's Supper closely to church membership as the meal of the church. The effect may be to play down ideas about it which might otherwise encourage us to welcome to the table those whom we might not feel able, in our tradition, to baptise because of the emphasis we place on responsibility. For example the Supper is a sign or promise of a banquet in God's Kingdom for all human kind. Can it remain as such if we refuse a place to the mentally 'halt' and 'lame' and 'blind' who ask to come? Would not the sign contradict the promise! Or again, the Supper is a means of grace by which God nourishes God's people, some would even say converts them. Do we deprive the mentally handicapped of its blessings, or allow them instead to enjoy its benefits?

4.   A strict and logical attitude to church membership and who is to be admitted should be the norm not the absolute rule, even where we are dealing with able people. How much more is it required of us not to be over rigidly consistent with those who fall outside the more familiar range of human experience?

5.   Whilst being careful not to misuse admittance to the church and the Lord's Supper in order to make points that we should be making abundantly clear in other, more appropriate ways (for example: that God loves us; that we are accepted however lacking in ability, virtue or attractiveness; that the Kingdom of God and the sphere of salvation embrace all sorts of surprising and unsuspecting people), we must be equally careful to ensure that exclusion from church membership and the Lord's Supper does not make precisely the wrong points to handicapped people of limited understanding. We must avoid, maybe at all costs, giving them the impression that God

doesn't want them and they are not welcome amongst God's people.

And so to my 'epilogue'. My seventeen year old daughter is mentally handicapped. Unlike her two older brothers who do not go to church, she attends happily with my wife and myself on Sunday mornings, and will even go off to an evening service by herself. In both cases people are friendly and make her welcome. We share in the Lord's Supper every Sunday and our custom is to stand in a circle and pass the loaf and cup round, serving one another. They pass Katie by. She would prefer them not to and asks why she cannot join in. During the week she is part of a special programme for handicapped young people in a local sixth-form college. It is a Roman Catholic foundation. She has been to Mass and according to her reports she has 'had it' like everybody else! She has also been present at the local swimming pool when several of our members were baptised. It wouldn't take a lot of encouragement for her to agree to be baptised as well. To add to these splendid ecumenical complications, our Baptist congregation has recently been joined by a United Reformed Church which allows children to share the communion so that Katie is doubly perplexed as to why she is left out.

I myself, and I think my wife, have generally resisted the gentle pressures from Katie and others for her to become, by baptism, a member of the church and take her full place at the table. Our two sons have also resisted it on the grounds that it would be exploiting her. The church would gain a convert by taking advantage of the fact that she did not know what she was doing. If she did, they assume that, like them, she would say 'No'. I dislike exploitation but I do not take their point very seriously. There would be little advantage to the church or disadvantage to Katie - two essential ingredients of exploitation; indeed Katie would probably feel that the church had done her a good turn!

I was not in favour of her joining for two main reasons. First I thought it meant trying to do the right thing in the wrong way. The right thing is to affirm that Katie is part of God's family, is loved by God, is acceptable to God and is part of God's coming Kingdom and on her way to being saved and completed. In these respects she is like everyone else in the world as far as I am concerned; but making her a member of the church by baptism and admitting her subsequently to the table is not the right way to affirm it, any more than it would be fitting to baptise everyone else. Such a misuse of church membership maybe reveals how bad we are as churches at making God's indiscriminate love and acceptance plain to those who don't belong, and at celebrating the signs of the Kingdom in their sorrow, perseverance and love.

My second reason had to do with my view of the church. I

react against the notion that the church is meant to be numerically large, indeed to embrace as many people as possible until in theory it contains the whole world. I believe the church is small, a testing vocation for the few. If large numbers join, it can only be that the invitations issued and accepted were based on a misunderstanding. The church, unlike God's love and salvation and God's Kingdom, is not for the general public but for disciples who learn to follow the costly way that redeems the world or at least saves it from the worst. Disciples of this kind, and here remarks made by my sons found echoes in my own view of the matter, need to know what they are doing. Kindness and sentiment are not enough. There must be understanding. It doesn't reach very great heights in the best of us. Could it even get off the ground with Katie? I more than doubted it. I had tried to explain relatively simple things to her in the past. I had spent hours, though only occasionally since my patience is short and my will weak, teaching her the meaning of a word, only to be back at square one the next morning. I knew that even what she did learn needed to be constantly reinforced, as if others had to keep alive in her what would never be of herself. I had to admit that she did learn: practical routines, skills, and how to read. She could surprise us. She did understand; but the level of sustained, conceptual understanding, which is not to be confused with being 'intellectual' or 'clever', was nowhere near what is required to be a disciple with intent to follow Christ.

From this admirably clear position, or so it seemed to me, I have moved to one which is less clear and more open to the possibility of Katie being baptised and joining the church if the church and Katie happily agree about it, and even to her being more fully involved in the Lord's Supper whether she is baptised or not. I like to believe it is for reasons referred to in this paper and that the effort to think through the whole issue has led to a genuine change of mind. I have to ask however what other forces could be at work. Am I for example rationalising my desire not to disappoint her? Am I being swayed by sentiments which might benefit her but not the good ordering of the church and therefore the many? Am I unwilling to face up to ecumenical discomfort which owes more to our Baptist teaching on believers' baptism than to any peculiar circumstances surrounding my daughter? I try to be aware of these influences even if I cannot wholly avoid them. They do not necessarily prove my tentative conclusions wrong. Neither do they encourage me to think that the question that was put to me is easily settled.

MICHAEL TAYLOR

SHOULD SHE BE ALLOWED?

The Church was hushed! Communion was being shared and there was a beautiful spirit of quiet participation. The cup had been "offered" and was now being passed, the musicians were quietly playing "Reach out and touch the Lord as He passes by", and each worshipper literally felt the desire to do just that, when suddenly a discordant, childish, slurring voice shattered the tranquillity with "Give Pauline drink". A teenage mentally handicapped child, sitting between her parents, had suddenly asserted her desire to share in Communion. Should she be allowed? Her father's question: "What is the Church's teaching about this?"

I must admit that when the question was first put to me my response was one of horror. Does the Church have to have a special "teaching", a "theological doctrine" on whether a mentally handicapped child is able to take Communion? But on reflection I have to confess that it is right that the Church should be expected to give guidance and teaching on such a deeply felt subject.

In approaching such matters let us first of all ask ourselves one or two very basic questions. Firstly, is a mentally handicapped child a whole human being or just half of one? Don't be horrified by the question and don't jump to conclusions. There are many cultures in the world that would answer "No - a mentally handicapped person is not a whole human being". Some animistic societies would see them as spirits (demons), seeking human form. Others would regard them as "soul-less" and therefore "less than human".My strong conviction is that just as a thalidomide victim is a whole human being despite a physical handicap, so too a mentally handicapped person is still a whole human being - for humanity does not depend on the quantity or quality of the constituent parts but rather the origin.

Then, secondly, is such a person "a child of God"? Would God have said to Jeremiah "Before I created you in the womb I knew you, and before you were born I consecrated you", if there had been the possibility of him being mentally handicapped? Caution... We often use those verses in order to assure each other of God's eternal care and concern. Not one of us is an accident as far as God is concerned no matter what our parents felt - but does that apply also to the mentally handicapped? Granted that it is not God's intention that anyone should be born mentally handicapped, any more than it is His intention that any imperfection should exist in His creation, but that imperfection having happened God does not then reject His child but rather seeks to redeem. And His acceptance of us does not depend upon our degree of perfection (be it spiritual, mental or physical), but upon His redeeming grace.

This being so then let me openly acknowledge that a mentally handicapped person is a human being in the fullest sense of the term and, as such, a child of God. Because of their handicap they may not be able to understand that fact, nor respond to it, but the degree of their understanding and response does not alter the fact. God loves them, Jesus died for them, the Holy Spirit seeks to embrace them – then so must the Church.

Does this mean that we are justified in evangelising the mentally handicapped? If by "evangelise" we mean reaching out to share God's love then, yes. As the minister of the Baptist Church in Gillingham I became involved in a centre started by one of our couples. They felt led to sink their savings, with the backing and help of the Church, in buying a large house and opening it to help in the rehabilitation of the mentally ill. This venture rapidly came to embrace the mentally handicapped and mentally damaged as well as the sick. Inevitably the love of this couple, and the Church as a whole, drew a response from a number of those so helped and we were faced with the question concerning Communion, baptism, membership, marriage and parenthood etc. Others within the Church were involved in other ways – a couple whose child is mentally handicapped; one couple who fosters and now is adopting children who are educationally subnormal, etc.

Obviously, each person is thought about, prayed about and treated individually, yet, nevertheless, I do believe that there can be teaching and doctrine that is theologically all-embracing.

Let us begin with our understanding of the child in the Church. Some years ago a major report came out within our Baptist Church concerning the Child and the Church and, if my memory has not failed me, the overriding conclusion of that report was that the child is as much a part of the Church as the white of an egg is part of the egg, and the child does not cease to be part of the Church until such time as he or she rejects Christ – in other words, a child is part of the Family until that child opts out. Now obviously, that needs spelling out and qualifying beyond the brief of this short comment but as a general principle let it stand. So our Service of Dedication is conducted in the midst of the Redeemed people of God, the Church, because the child is seen to be part of that Company, although not being aware of it except experientially.

When children are able to discern what God has done in them, and respond, then we say that they have made a personal commitment and themselves opt to be part of the Family of God. At what point/age/stage that discernment is reached is a matter for ongoing debate, but until that point, generally speaking, the Church embraces them within the Family. So parents love to hear a child of three saying her prayers and acknowledging her love for Jesus. The

Church "coos" in loving, harmonious response.

What then of the person who can never mentally develop beyond the age of three? Are they "theologically" so very different? The adults who are so unkindly dubbed "cabbage" - are they arbitrarily excluded from the Kingdom? I sincerely believe not. In the first instance such a person is part of the Family and must be loved as such. Secondly, if in their limited way they are ever able to communicate a response to what they experience of God's love then they must be nurtured, encouraged and enabled in every way to make that response. This must mean that the Communion Table is open to them - however inadequate their ability to express their faith. It must also mean that some will be enabled to express further their response in baptism if such is their desire - no matter how little they grasp the theological implications. It naturally follows that Discipleship Classes must be sensitive and simple in the extreme - but to understand that God loves them, that Jesus died for them and to want to respond positively to that grace must surely open the door to their total acceptance.

TOM ROGERS

WITH UNDERSTANDING

What Clare understands by the term 'fellowship' I do not really know, but she associates it mainly with the Communion. Similarly, she has asked me, 'Is it the Blood tonight, Dad?' It seems that certain words in the context of the sacrament have registered and she uses the single words as representing the whole. If we ask what she means, her immediate reaction is 'I don't know'. She uses words, knows what *she* means and often uses them in the correct context, but to ask her to elucidate what she says, takes too much 'brain power'.

Clearly Clare likes to go to church. The church people make a fuss of her and there are a few who have become special friends. It could be that seeing everyone around her taking Communion she did not want to feel left out. Perhaps she enjoys the wine! In all this we are guessing. For Clare, going to church is a 'being together' with friends. Similarly when her brothers are at home she has remarked 'We are a family'. She perceives a 'togetherness' which is more complete than when only parents and daughter are present.

Should she be admitted to the Church through Baptism, or to the Lord's Table? I think that, on the whole, such sacraments are only helpful for those who have some real appreciation of what they mean. They need to *understand* that:

a) They are ordinances of the Lord

b) They require a modicum of personal experience and understanding of the Lord Jesus Christ as Son of God and Saviour

c) Plus a belief in the work of the Holy Spirit to use the elements of Bread, Wine and Water to impart real grace

d) That what we do is in some way (not easily defined) as 'necessary', 'essential', so that if we ignore them or misuse them something 'spiritual' will be lacking.

Baptism and Communion, and its antecedent Church Membership, require some *real* ability to respond intellectually, that is, to comprehend what is involved. If not, we are back to a magical idea where certain things - here water, bread, wine - help because of what they are, whether we understand or are ready or fit to receive them. In order to keep these matters real and vital for the participants and to maintain a level of spiritual integrity, we need to hold fast to the need for real faith and understanding of what we are doing in the sacraments.

I would not let Clare be baptised at the moment. She does not need it. She is incapable really of sinning or of understanding sin or any need of Christ or Salvation. God in His grace blesses her abundantly now. Only if I accepted the water through ministerial blessing became a cleansing medium or something magical to do something to her that the water alone could do, would I feel the need to baptise her. Baptism requires faith and understanding in some degree to be effective.

The Communion is different. I don't suppose for a moment it helps her specifically - but she wants to do what all the others are doing around her.

Open membership I accept as an accommodation to an ecumenical need. It is often 'irregular' - as is the Open Table - but the Closed approach is even more so. We live in a world where black and white areas are impossible to define accurately and impossible to maintain.

GEORGE NEAL

54

WHERE MINISTERS FEAR TO TREAD

Some lay thoughts

The Baptist Union Working Group on Mental Handicap and the Church began with matters of pastoral concern, Christian education, and community service, but has come to realise that these are not enough. There is a real need to think about what we believe.

There are two main areas demanding theological thought:

How we understand mental handicap within God's scheme of creation. Why does it happen? How do we see the mentally handicapped themselves?

How we see baptism, communion, and church membership in relation to the mentally handicapped. This presents special problems for Baptists, who emphasise personal, mature understanding.

It is perhaps tempting to dodge the first area, to skate round unanswerable questions, but unless we face up to those it is hardly possible to look properly at the area of church and sacraments. The better we come to terms with all these questions, the better equipped we shall be to help the mentally handicapped and their families.

* * * * * * * *

How do we understand mental handicap within God's creation?

Families whose newborn baby has serious mental handicap will have a tangle of emotions: love, rejection, guilt, fear of the unknown, isolation from normal society. Here is a planned, wanted, prayed-over baby born into a loving Christian home - but, alas, creation has gone wrong.

What has the minister to say in that situation? All too often, nothing. Pastoral care can be good, and yet the minister may not touch on matters that certainly trouble some parents. Lay people who would never be found reading theology for 'general interest' may think deeply when faced with such a crisis. Those parents may long to talk and yet find it impossible to broach theological questions if they feel the minister would prefer to avoid such complexities.

But where ministers fear to tread, others will rush in. They will ensure parents ask why it happens. They will suggest some answers.

If our faith is part of our lives, of our daily living, we have to come to terms with the question 'Why?'. Some parents find this much easier than others. For some it is hardly an issue at all. Some will derive great comfort from understandings which others find inadequate. Some will wrestle for weeks, months, years even, clinging tenuously to faith, before they can make any sense of it. Mental handicap can be critical: in the face of it marriages founder, faith is lost. Yet other families seem to thrive on adversity: the happiness of their homes, the brightness of their Christian witness is enhanced. They are held up as shining examples.

Lots of factors are involved, but I expect that the parents with a success story, in spite of or because of the handicap, will have found some answer to that 'Why?' which makes sense to them.

Injury and disease may prompt similar questions, but there is something particularly difficult about random genetic failure to reproduce in the normal human pattern. It is harder to attribute blame to human misjudgement or misuse of the environment. To say - as some do - 'it is part of Original Sin' is little help to parents who see their friends with normal children while their own baby embarks on life with curtailed hopes. That at least was our experience. We were in our late twenties when our son was born mentally handicapped. Over the previous decade we had between us lost three parents, through multiple sclerosis, leukaemia and road accident, and severe illness had left my husband with permanent physical handicap. These were not easy things to come to terms with, but none of them made the assault on our faith that our son's condition did.

So - _Why does it happen?_   There seem to be three main approaches.

The fatalistic - accepting that whatever will be, will be. Resigning oneself to the blows of fate and just getting on with life unquestioning has a certain appeal, but it is not easy for Christians to settle for 'blind fate'. Resignation may come a little easier for those parents who for some reason (e.g. age) accepted before conception a higher risk of a defective child.

Everything is sent from God, in his wisdom, for a purpose
'God', as a young crippled woman explained, 'makes some people handicapped to be good for the able-bodied'. It is asserted that God deliberately chooses people for the privilege of bearing and rearing a special child. Good Christian parents are comforted with the thought that they were chosen as able to cope with this special gift. Not too many questions are asked about all those other families, with marriages already under strain and no sustaining faith.

I myself find this approach untenable, so I am a poor advocate for it, although I have to recognise it as a valid view, in which many parents find comfort.

In Joni's film 'Blessings out of Brokenness', the mother of two multiply-handicapped children bears her testimony. It is a rather giggly, nervous presentation but commands respect. In it she declares, 'I don't have any problems with the sovereignty of God: I know He's to blame for it all'. And her faith still shines out. It was the ripple of laughter that ran round a Christian audience that left me stunned. If a mother can believe that and still worship God, it is not something to laugh about.

The most salutary letter of sympathy we received after Richard's birth was from a minister's wife, saying 'I know how you must hate God'. It was salutary because my anger at the suggestion made me realise that amid all the anguish and questioning it had not occurred to us to hate God: we could not feel He was to blame. Surely God intended creation to be good, to go right! I find it impossible to believe that God deliberately miscreates. That is why I prefer a third explanation.

Things go wrong because of the power of evil in the world, but the love of God can prevail. Belief in the devil may be old-fashioned but it is hardly unscriptural! An anthropomorphic concept of evil is for some still as helpful as an anthropomorphic view of God.

We recognised that to 'blame the devil' raised potentially tricky questions about the omnipotence of God, but initially found it easier to worship a loving than an omnipotent, uncaring God. It took time to see beyond that apparent choice. Evil exists, but the Lord is able to take the bad, the things that have gone wrong, and bring forth good. Is not that the mark of sovereignty? The devil has the power to strike where it will hurt most, but out of the depths we can still call with confidence upon God's all-sufficient grace. Voicing this aloud has revealed that this view is held quite widely - often a bit sheepishly.

Whichever approach one adopts there are theological difficulties. My present concern is not to decide between these, or other understandings, but to show that the individual has to come to terms with 'Why?' in some way that makes sense to him if faith is to survive. Most lay people get along all right without much thought for theology, but when forced to take stock of what we believe we should not waste the crisis. It can deepen our faith and enhance our witness.

Some Christians see God as a shield and protector, a guard against disaster (Psalm 91.9-11). Others are more aware of faith as an 'oaken staff', of God as a very present help in trouble, ('If I make my bed in hell, behold, Thou art there ... even there shall Thy hand lead me', Psalm 139,8-10). The understandings are not mutually exclusive, but they may make enormous difference to how people bear adversity.

Many parents really do struggle with such questions. Two ministers, writing about the experience of families in their churches, have observed this. 'They have been through the questions such as - Why has this happened? Why did God allow it? The questions now are more practical'. 'The handicapped child has caused much heart-searching and even doubts about a simplistic fundamentalist faith, yet at the end of the day what emerges is a more assured, developed faith in the providence of an Almighty God'.

This is something ministers need to recognise. The individual may have to wrestle with it for himself, but the minister should be alert for the search for understanding. Unless some acceptable understanding is achieved - and some find this so much easier than others - the family is unlikely to continue in the church, especially with all the extra difficulties of frequent illness and unsocial behaviour that attach to mental handicap. We cannot afford to evade the impossible question: Why does it happen?

How do we see the mentally handicapped?

Are they really human? Yes, of course - but do we always think so? Is that how we treat them? Or do we really see them as sub-human? The most severely handicapped are often spoken of as 'cabbages'. People see them as almost more vegetable than animal. Some, indeed, are barely animate. Does this mean they are beyond God's love? Surely not, although it is very hard to know how it can be made known to them.

Some people like the idea that the mentally handicapped are God's holy innocents who will never know sin, 'angels unawares', 'heavenly Peter Pans'. This line is often, very kindly, offered to parents. It denies the handicapped full humanity. Imagine the joy of realising that your child is knowingly, deliberately being naughty! It is a sign of recognisably human understanding. Between mothers of the subnormal such instances are shared as developmental milestones. Some parents never get that reassurance.

Childlike in some ways, the mentally handicapped may like children qualify as the very stuff of the Kingdom. They bear prophetic witness to values which we in our materialistic, competitive way of life easily overlook. Nevertheless, we must not get too sentimental about it. We undervalue the mentally handicapped if we fail to recognise such understanding as they have. Many are capable of feeling guilt when they do something wrong, when they hurt others. To deny this erodes their humanity.

Communication can be very difficult, yet even the profoundly handicapped may be touched by love, gentleness, peace. Often those for whom words have limited meaning will be sensitive to atmosphere. Those who work among them stress how important it is to live out their faith if they are to communicate anything of it. Roman Catholics and Anglicans concerned with the mentally handicapped stress that love, not intellect, is the focal point of Christianity. We would hardly argue with that. They suggest that anyone capable of loving *or of receiving love* is capable of religious experience. That qualification takes us a long way down the IQ scale. 'No sense, No feeling?' asked the Mencap advertisement. 'They may not think as fast, but they feel as deeply'. Spirituality surely has as much to do with feeling as with thinking. People with very limited intelligence are capable of worshipping God.

We must not begrudge the mentally handicapped a share in our humanity. We have to see that they too are of value in God's sight, the objects of God's love. Like other disadvantaged people, the poor, the sick, the outcast, they should be the concern of the followers of Christ.

* * * * * * * *

How do we see the mentally handicapped in relation to the church?

A subject for Christian concern? Yes, indeed. Candidates for church membership? Is that another matter? It has to be rather easier for paedobaptists, who see their children, however handicapped, baptised into the church. Confirmation may, or may not, follow, but they are within, they have received the seed of faith, they belong. Baptists are often not too sure where normal children stand in relation to the church family, let alone those whose mental age will never advance beyond childhood.

The Dedication service is not usually a problem. Should it be - if we have doubts about their future place in the church? Normally we come in thanksgiving for the gift of new life, to dedicate parents and church to rear the child in the knowledge and love of God, and to pray that in fulness of time he will embrace the faith for himself. When we bring a defective child, the thanksgiving may be a bit muted, and there will be overshadowing doubts about the child ever becoming *capable* of personal knowledge of Christ.

We brought our second son, five weeks old and with Down's Syndrome, with very different feelings from those with which we presented our first child three years earlier. The lively sense of hope for the future was gone. In its place was not emptiness, but something that went deeper. For us that dedication was an act of acceptance of the child we had. We prayed that God would make his life worthwhile, even if not in the ways we might have wished. Most of the churchmembers, though not the congregation at large, were aware of the baby's condition. A visiting American minister told me afterwards he had never before found a dedication service so moving. Without knowing the special reason, he had sensed the involvement of the church. It did not seem to us mere coincidence when that day Richard produced his first real smiles. It felt as though that service had brought him to life as a person, not just a defective baby. Over the years since, Richard has enjoyed more freedom and independence, and responsibilities too, at church than anywhere else. This has been possible because from the first the church took on a corporate responsibility for this child in very real, and practical, ways.

Some of the mentally handicapped are so severely disturbed or so multiply handicapped that they will not be brought to church. We must not forget them, and the need of Christian parents to be sure that their child too has a place in God's love, if not in the local church.

Others are able to come with their families. They grow up through the Sunday School classes, although often dropping behind their own age group, which presents its own problems. In some ways their minds will never cease to be 'as little children's', but in other respects they do grow up. Their experience of life is not that of a little child.

For many mentally handicapped people the local church may be the only 'normal' community into which they are integrated. This in itself can make the church very important in their lives. This being so, we have to ask whether we see the mentally handicapped as potential candidates for baptism, for church membership, for communion. Answers vary; and they vary in principle, not just for individual cases.

The mentally handicapped have little grasp of abstract concepts. This, however, need not prevent them from knowing Christ. They can picture Jesus. He may be invisible, but Christ Incarnate is not an abstraction. Many mentally handicapped men and women know Jesus as a personal friend.

Baptism

Can the mentally handicapped have that sense of conviction, of personal response that Baptists require for believer's baptism? How do we know how much they understand? Some will be more articulate than others, but they are unlikely to express themselves quite like other candidates. If they do, we probably have to ask whether the sentiments, as well as the vocabulary, are second-hand.

To accept a young person of limited understanding for baptism because he belongs to a Christian family and enjoys coming to church would be coming uncomfortably close to accepting the parents' faith as proxy. Proxy faith is not easy for Baptists! To refuse to recognise him as fully part of the fellowship of which he feels a member may be unrealistic, and, indeed, cruel.

Ministers and churches differ in their response when faced with such a question. Many gladly welcome the handicapped brother or sister, eager to demonstrate that God's love is for all. Others assert, albeit with regret, that they would not understand about baptism and church membership. They demand a level of intellectual competence, which sounds reasonable, yet however stringent 'election' may be, it seems unlikely to involve an intelligence test.

Various suggestions have been made to me recently for assessing the readiness of a mentally handicapped youth, like my own son, for baptism. Is he capable of feeling guilt? Is he capable of resisting going to church, like a normal teenager? Apart from reflecting that we evidently have two abnormal sons, I find this a horribly negative approach. I want to ask positive questions: Is there evidence that he loves God? Does he care about other people? Is Christ real to him?

Church Membership

If a mentally handicapped person seeks baptism, is it the baptism we find difficult, or do problems arise because baptism normally leads to church membership. We find it hard to envisage our mentally handicapped friends as church members. They may put up hymn numbers or wash coffee cups, but take part in the sacred business of decision making in Church Meeting? Ah, there's the rub: they would not understand.

There is a tendency, when we consider the mentally handicapped as possible church members, to assess them by ideal standards of how we see the church. I do not believe we do this to normal candidates. In this context, some point out that we do not remove from our church rolls those members who have become senile, but I am not only thinking of them. Most churches have some members who may be regular in worship but play no other active part in church life.

Those mentally handicapped people who are church members and choose to attend Church Meetings will mostly sit passive, yet it may be important to be present, to belong, to add their 'Amen', to be spoken to before and after the meeting. Of course, there will be the odd 'difficult' one who wants to have his say, which will not advance the business very fast. That kind of contribution does not come exclusively from the handicapped. The risk of an irrelevant interruption is a poor reason for excluding all the mentally handicapped from the body of Christ. Before we deny church membership to those mentally handicapped men and women for whom it would have some meaning, however limited, we need to ask searching questions about our understanding of the church.

Traditionally it has been participation at the Lord's Table, rather than at Church Meeting, that has been the essential requirement for continuing membership. So what about the mentally handicapped there?

Communion

Our mentally handicapped friends may have joined lustily, if untunefully, in the hymns, they may have listened intently to the sermon, or sat silent, or fidgety, barely sharing in the service that has preceded the Communion. Here at last is something they can grasp. We Baptists, for our own good reasons, are short on audio-visual aids. We have not cared much for symbols, for rituals, for 'empty' repetitions. We love the Word. And that is hard on those who find words difficult. The mentally handicapped like things they can see, and touch, and feel. They value repetition. They welcome pictures and symbols. We do not have much to offer in that way, but we have Baptism and we have the Lord's Table. If the church is part of their lives, these will be important, especially the regularly repeated act of communion. Are they welcome there? Not always.

How many of us really grasp the full significance of the sacrament? Can it be appropriate to bar the mentally handicapped from the Lord's Table once they grasp it is Jesus's party from which they are excluded? We may be startled by the report of one mentally handicapped woman on first receiving communion, 'It was drinks all round at church today!', but she understands *something* of the communion celebration.

How does this relate to baptism and membership? We expect to look to baptism, church membership, communion: in that order. It seems logical, but it does not always work out so tidily, even with normal people. With the mentally handicapped, especially when baptisms are occasional rather than frequent events, the crunch questions may well arise over communion. They will often come in the first instance to the parents sitting next to their mentally handicapped son or daughter in the pew.

My husband and I would have preferred to have discussed this with minister and church in advance, but we were taken by surprise, well before we had expected it to arise. We permitted an intuitive response, but uneasily, aware of the theological implications. One Sunday, in a distant church, Richard heard the invitation to all who love the Lord Jesus Christ. He clearly interpreted that as including him. We did not, and my husband passed the plate across Richard to me. The expression on Richard's face shook us both: not just disappointment, but real hurt. There was no prospect of him understanding explanations afterwards. 'Forbid him not' came so clearly that on the spur of the moment I split my crumb in two and took half a sip, passing the rest to Richard. Seeing how much it meant to him, we felt this had been right, once Richard had taken in that open invitation. The decision had to be taken on the spot. Having once begun, partaking could not come and go. Richard has shared in communion ever since, where the invitation is simply to those who love the Lord Jesus. We feel uneasy about him taking communion without baptism, yet he loves Jesus and feels very much part of the church. He was only thirteen when this arose - yet it was the point when he no longer saw himself as a child. For him it was part of growing up, in the church context. But is that enough? We Baptists cannot stand aside from other Christian brethren over our understanding of believer's baptism and of the church and then take a casual attitude to personal response and responsibility.

It is likely that the sense of belonging - or of being left out - will be most acute at the Lord's Table. We cannot, however, divorce communion from baptism and church membership. We must be concerned to treat holy things seriously. That need not rule out simple faith: the mentally handicapped may grasp less, but still grasp what matters. Limited understanding need not mean lack of reverence. The local church may feel it is right to be generous about this, raise no objections, even take a certain pride in welcoming the handicapped to the fold. Often it is the parents whom the implications trouble. Much of the responsibility of understanding and interpreting the handicapped son or daughter lies with them. Is this child more easily steered to conform to their ways? They would love him to share their faith - but can they be sure he does?

Some mentally handicapped people are able to assert their wish to belong. Others may feel part of the church but be unable to express this. Others are beyond any personal response. Parents want to know where their loved child stands in relation to Christ and the church. Is he left outside? Not all parents understand the principles involved. Baptist church members do not all fully grasp the distinctive Baptist understandings about the nature of the church. They may see denial of a place in the church as denial of a place in the Kingdom. At best it will not be very reassuring.

There are issues of principle and theology at stake here. At present they are resolved only at local level, according to the instincts and understanding of the local minister, the local fellowship, the parents. Individual cases must always be decided at this level, but wider consideration of the matter might provide useful guidance.

Let us not too readily assume that the mentally handicapped cannot understand. Let us not write them off as only candidates for the church's pastoral concern, desirable though that is. People of very low IQ can worship God. They can find in Jesus a friend who actually understands them.

We may regret mental handicap, but we must accept the mentally handicapped for their own sake as precious in God's sight. We must not, with our thought-out structures, make it harder for them to know the love of God.

FAITH BOWERS

THE SACRAMENTS AND PEOPLE WITH MENTAL HANDICAP*

I am a full-time Anglican Chaplain at a local hospital, catering for mentally handicapped adults over 16 years, with almost 500 residents of varying abilities and handicaps. All are mentally and socially retarded in some way and they require a sheltered community for some time. We have our own Church building called St Francis and the ministry has been ecumenical with Anglican and Free Church Chaplains serving together in worship and pastoral care for fifteen years. The main Sunday Holy Communion is based on an adapted Series 3 form. There are also weekly Fellowship and Prayer Services and shortened Holy Communion 'Happenings' in Homes for the elderly and the more severely handicapped who are unable to get to Sunday worship. [1]

I want to describe and reflect on some of the sacramental worship in this setting where it is particularly adapted to the mentally handicapped. I also want to indicate how this worship

*   *This is an extended version of an article originally published in Liturgy 9/5, 1985. Reproduced by kind permission of the Roman Catholic Bishops' Conference of England and Wales Liturgy Office.*

matches and meets their human and spiritual needs. This will then
enable me to draw out aspects that can be generalised in the local
Church. The issues of Baptism, preparation for membership and
admission to Holy Communion will also be raised.

A. Reflections on the Sunday Eucharist

About 50 or 60 people of all abilities meet for this. Some are brought
by staff and volunteers, some come in wheelchairs. There is a choir,
there are stewards and helpers and a lady cross-bearer. One
resident is a helper to the Organist. Before the Service starts there
is anticipation, greeting and welcome. The residents come without
making a distinction between life and worship and will greet someone
in an act of common humanity whether you are singing a hymn or
not! We shake hands or hug one another as a means of greeting
because worship is being with friends. Being together is the
bed-rock of our worship and experience. In this way we 'slip' into
worship. There are two aspects of our worship: [2]

(1) **The first phase** consists of short items; participation is
encouraged with short hymns, action-songs and a reading. The talk
that follows seeks to articulate and involve. Residents are
encouraged to take part in the action of the talk through drama and
mime or help in the visual aid. Those without speech can share in
this by clapping or joining in the actions and grasp intuitively the
symbolic content. Everyone feels part of the action. Their
contribution is acknowledged and accepted in a positive way, where
a lady shouts out in the talk 'I am fed up' or another concludes the
talk by saying 'Yes, Jesus loves us all, doesn't he, Mr Easter'. So
there are the elements of rumbustiousness, freedom and intuition.
Out of apparent weakness comes joy and exhilaration. The colour,
the pictures round the Church, the music, all combine to produce a
visual symbolic feast, with the enjoyment of Christ, our Friend, at
the centre. [3]

(2) **The second aspect** which focuses on the Holy Communion involves
a change in pace and tone. It moves to a climax that again requires
participation: in coming to the communion rail; bringing a friend,
helping along a more severely handicapped person; greeting others
as we meet and joining in the Eucharistic Shout 'Lift Up Your
Hearts'. Anticipation and a sense of wonder pervades the whole
Service. Everything is thanksgiving, not only the words of
institution, it is a *total* experience. A sense of belonging is very
intense. No-one who is present is refused communion. We encourage
an 'open table' regardless of a person's handicap; their being with
us is sufficient qualification to receive.

Over the years central themes have arisen reflecting the
worship-experience of the residents:

(a) This total thanksgiving becomes a *Drama* in which we are all involved. [4] We are caught up in the pattern of words and actions that we know well, that moves to a climax and de-escalates after receiving the communion. We know this pattern well and we feel part of it. It is a positive ritual experience that gives room for variation, that is open to adaptation to the congregation and to Christ by his Spirit. The element of anticipation and repetition is important. This Drama is a *recital* of God's loving action towards us that draws us to Him through it. No-one is excluded from this experience. The building, the pictures and the actions that demonstrate God's great Drama make our small Dramas important. The repetition of what we know well is a deep element in the life of mentally handicapped people. There is *recapitulation* here, too. The Drama is more than a mere reminder; we actually re-live by the words, actions and music, the Gospel happenings and the Biblical story. We are in the Upper Room. This imaginative leap is taken by the residents with wonder and joy. They know they are with Jesus Christ and He is with them through these tangible things. Direct, simple, symbolic action makes present the past. All these dramatic elements mean that everyone has a part to play; all are incorporated in the story and therefore are significant and are wanted. [5]

(b) In the Eucharist Christ *offers* himself to us. It is an objective sign given by God, that depends for its effectiveness on Him, apart from our weakness, failures and handicaps. The ritual actions assure us that God is there regardless of our feelings, according to promise: 'This is my body'. He is our faithful friend, keeping His word. The residents want to be sure about that. For them the sacrament is an 'effectual sign', 'a means whereby God leads us to himself by these earthly elements' (J. Calvin). I attempt to demonstrate God's offer by holding out across the Table the Cup and the Bread. [6]

(c) It is a visible *Exhibition* of God's love, Christ's death and resurrection, our forgiveness and acceptance. That we are 'wanted' is pictured in the most powerful and life-like symbolism. The congregation intuitively understand love-in-action, being hurt, real friendship. It is all shown in living tangible terms through people and signs. They may not grasp abstractions but delight in this. Like Bill who comes to receive with a radiant smile, bows his head, then offers the Chaplain a sweet. Isn't this grasping what it all represents?! This leads to -

(d) *Encounter with the Living God.* Janet says 'Thank you, God' as she receives. It is for her an occasion for personal meeting. All the structures, forms, words, music, actions and signs are means towards *this* - the mystery of encounter. This is not an isolated thing, it is *with* others in the enjoyment of others. A volunteer brings two residents holding hands on each side. They keep holding hands as they receive, demonstrating a mutual encounter with God. Is not the communion 'a participation with Christ'?[7]

(e) An occasion for *Divine Accommodation*. In the Eucharist God adapts himself as a good father to his children's needs. The residents do not need to reach up and out of themselves to contact Him. He comes and touches and speaks in *their* terms. In the Incarnation He comes in our flesh. In the Eucharist the incarnate Lord comes by his Spirit in our words, our signs, in our 'world' in a total *embodied* way. He comes alongside us, inviting us, as we are, to His friendship meal. The residents can grasp eating, drinking, a meal, a party, being together. As Jane put it in a Home Communion: 'Jesus - party - bread and jam - Mummy' - a whole undivided world! Here everything *fits* for them because God has arranged it so. The redemptive, natural and the personal coalesce as a reality 'we know'.[8]

(f) *The Reality of Participation.* This has several elements combining to induce lively and moving results for us all:

(i) A kinetic experience. We are drawn into the Service whether or not we can read or speak. We participate by doing, by action. As Richard struggles to get to the communion rail with his walking aid rather than sit in his seat. Others come early to be in the front seats to be 'in' on the action. Marjorie lifts and opens her arms in welcome as the Ministers bring the communion to her chair. It is not a narrowly intellectual experience, nor a 'spiritual' out of the body one, but a whole-souled, whole-person event.

(ii) A social experience. The residents want to be together as part of the action with others. They help others participate - helping someone clap, to put hands together in prayer, find a page in a hymn book. Or to point out to Ministers someone who has not yet received. We grow and develop by interaction, in the sphere of the 'interhuman' (M. Buber). Isn't this New Testament *koinonia*? pointing back to the reality of being in God's image together and sharing redemption together?[9]

(iii) An ecstatic experience. Something dynamic, that reaches from rest to the reality of God's loving presence (ex-static). The residents reach out in joy and delight as they sing, laugh, move and pray. Bill groans and moves forward in his chair, in a reaching arc, as we sing or he prepares for communion. One of our favourite choruses has an action with open arms and head lifted upwards to symbolise this *sursum corda*.[10]

(iv) A dignifying experience. Here they know they are wanted for themselves not as the handicapped but, with staff and volunteers, God's people and friends. His greatest gift is for *them*. The body and blood of Christ is 'for you'. The bread and wine are broken 'for me'. Together we share in and are dignified by the humanity, love and glory of Jesus Christ. 'No one else may seem to bother with me, here I know He does. All the other people that care for me do it with His help. I know that I am worth something. I am wanted and accepted through what is happening *here* .[11]

B.   Theological and Practical Implications

(i)   For *understanding* in Holy Communion and Worship.

The residents 'understand' what is happening in their own terms, by being part of the potent ritual action. The signs and symbols have a *'condensed'* power - a depth and richness that can contain and mean something for everyone at a profound level. They are available to be grasped at our own appropriate level of understanding in a particular situation, depending on how 'I' am today. Anthropologists indicate too that symbols are *multivocal* - speaking to all participants in a way they can grasp.[12]

In appreciating worship with the St Francis' congregation I began with too narrow a view of understanding as parallel to 'abstract reasoning'. Now I am convinced that this finds its place in the wider experience of understanding by involvement. Finding meaning in, with and through action. This 'kinetic understanding' develops as we learn and grasp people and situations by presence and action. This is the case for all of us regarding spiritual realities, as when Christ speaks of 'doing' the truth to learn it.[13]

In worship and the life-setting it means widening *faith* to be more than assent to given information (an intellectual comprehension) but also *fiducia,* a heart trust and a commitment (a whole-person movement to Another). We grasp the other Person with the hand of the heart, 'feed on him in your hearts by faith'. Knowledge and understanding are 'total' things and in biblical terms are born in relationships.[14]

'Understanding' also means that in the Sacrament the residents face the mystery of the inter-personal. They meet the life-long Friend they know in other settings. They may not be able to put this mystery into words or express it fully, but they can *know* it and *understand* it. This is the case for all real and profound life-experience. 'I know it is happening but words can't fully express it'. For all of us, words, signs, gestures are inadequate but reliable pointers to final reality. We will not ever fully comprehend the heart of the Sacrament, we can only apprehend - grasp with faith. The narrowly intellectual cannot, in principle, be the criteria for experiencing, or admission to, the Sacrament, but the reality of being accepted, wanted and loved as a recipient of grace. As John Calvin expressed this sacramental understanding, 'What our mind does not comprehend, let faith conceive'.[15]

(2) *Union with Christ* in the Sacrament.

This experience is not only tangibly interhuman it also involves an 'inward and spiritual grace'. It is not only a question of our readiness but God's grasp of us in our totality. In sacramental communication the Holy Spirit's presence makes Christ real to us, invites us to Him - this is his secret and hidden work, pointed to in the 'Epiclesis'. He lifts the residents into union with Christ and into spiritual understanding. He is the cohesion between our flesh and Christ's flesh in the Eucharist as we are united to Him. The Spirit makes it easy for us all to come to Christ - for our hearts and hands to embrace Him. In biblical terms real understanding and wisdom is coming in this vulnerability and openness that is born of the Spirit. Likewise foolishness, lack of understanding, stupidity is not mental handicap (a question of level of intellect) but a *spiritual* matter - being proud, self-contained, self-reliant and disobedient. My friends at St Francis constantly remind me of this as they are drawn to God. I can never forget the Spirit who leads them gently to Christ.[16]

(3) The *purpose* of the Sacrament.

The Fathers, Cranmer and Calvin among others, speak of the Eucharist as 'medicine for the sick, bread for the hungry and needy', to encourage the hesitant and those who feel least acceptable. It is not for the healthy or strong but for the *weak*. Not for the *perfect* but the feeble. Here healing is found for the weak, the sinner, the stumbling, inadequate and disabled. Here they may find renewal, quickening strength and know they are loved. The Sacrament is ordained for the vulnerable, dependent and helpless. This is why we invite and encourage *all* the residents. In their dependent receptivity they fully qualify! The Sacrament thus demonstrates the heart of the Gospel of Grace to them.[17]

(4) The *relationship* of the mentally handicapped to God.

As their ministers, our inclusion of all the residents reflects our conviction that this service and the Gospel asserts their participation in the *image* of God by virtue of their existence, humanity, openness and utter dependence. If God has made them his covenant children and united them to Christ to share His redemption, who can refuse them? This is demonstrated in their baptism into Christ and His Church, they are part of the family of God and are fellow-pilgrims on the road with us. Baptism is the complete qualification for their coming to Holy Communion by declaring God's free acceptance and their share in Christ's total work.

At St Francis we welcome the confirmed and the unconfirmed in our ecumenical setting. Baptism and being present is *the* qualification. [18]

C. The Local Church Setting

The same spiritual realities and theological principles are the case in the local Church as in the special community. People with mental handicap share with all other Christians the realities of union with Christ, creation in God's image, a faith-understanding of God's redeeming love, and a grace-right to equality in, and full membership of, the local fellowship. The criteria is not their level of handicap, but the reality of Christ's acceptance of them, and their covenantal right to all the means of grace. The issue is not about them having rights to come to the Sacrament but the practical one - how can the fellowship find the means to encourage, enrich and articulate that coming in love and understanding? There are one or two 'leads' out of our experience that may help.

1. *A natural and warm welcome* is crucial. Mentally handicapped people are particularly sensitive to the genuineness and warmth of a social environment. Our welcome to worship and the Lord's Table reflects *His* welcome to his children. Like us they need to be sincerely wanted and liked *for themselves,* this the gracious accommodation of the Sacrament demonstrates and can be expressed in our friendly and open attitude, however brokenly. People with communication difficulties or physical handicaps are immensely tolerant as long as they know our intention is real, that we want them with us in the awareness of being a poorer fellowship without them. This is sensed and appraised at a deep interpersonal level. [19]

2. *A genuine and real link* with each person's whole family is important. Or, if there is no family, with the home or hostel in which he or she lives. Human contact, shared friendship and care expresses that common humanity in Christ which, as we saw earlier, forms with the bread and wine the foundation and raw materials of our Eucharist or Thanksgiving. Being together through natural and appropriate friendship in worship, and out of it, can help the handicapped person through fear, failure and bereavements, and in the sharing of triumphs and joys. Sensitive pastoral care mirrors Christ's sacramental welcome and loving embrace. [20]

3. This welcome and care is particularly focussed in the *minister and the lay leadership.* Together, by living example and positive

understanding, they are particularly well placed to offer Christ's sacramental welcome to his children and demonstrate it to the whole congregation. This can be articulated graphically by actions and words. As mentally handicapped people and their families often indicate, the attitudes of Church leaders massively effect their feeling wanted, and whether they continue attending that particular Church.

The minister's attitude, gestures, facial expressions, tone of voice throughout the whole act of worship is an important encouragement especially if he or she is really enjoying the worship, and evidently enjoys having the handicapped present as natural and rightful contributors. This depends a great deal on the amount and quality of their experience of the mentally handicapped as people and friends. (Increasingly ministerial students are given positive opportunities for this during training). If the minister is clearly not put off by their presence, and there is not merely an uneasy tolerance but they are actively made part of the worship drama then this speaks volumes! Further, this positive acknowledgement of their contribution, clapping, shouting out, or singing either during the sermon or at other times, relaxes their relatives and assists the kinetic-participating element mentioned earlier. Again, where a person (in wheelchair or not) is encouraged to sit is crucial in terms of actual hearing or seeing and being included in 'the action', rather than pushed to the edge or a corner. Clarity of diction, positive acknowledgement of individual expressions of love or trust in God and a more direct physical exhibition of the bread and wine are also helpful, reflecting an inclusive catholicity that knows no bounds. Certainly, a great deal of so-called 'difficult behaviour' in church arises from the child or person not being acknowledged there, on their wanting to be 'free' in God's house. There is very often little need to assert oneself if that person feels amongst friends and equals, and is understood and accepted with minimum critical comment. [21]

More often, the active presence of people with mental handicap forces a congregation back to the basics of sacramental worship and fellowship, and enriches their life together - finding through them and their re-appraisals the truth of Stephen Winward's words, 'participation is the secret of interest'. [22]

4.   *Preparation for and experience of full membership.*

As indicated earlier, by God's grace and his Spirit, people with mental handicap have an intuitive faith-understanding of Christ, revealing this in involvement and action. In the local Church membership preparation can be the means of drawing out, enriching and assisting their articulation of that experience. It can be with others in the preparation-group or, according to need, in personal preparation. The preparation is best essentially action-orientated in learning about the sacramental actions, and their meaning. Songs to learn and pictures to remember are helpful too. Bradford's recommendation of a 'friend-tutor' to assist the candidate by understanding and consistency is an excellent one, not only before but after membership, providing special opportunities for guidance and explanation. [23]

All handicapped people appreciate a dignified and 'natural' reception into membership and will respond positively to the ritual aspects. Alongside this a fellowship group or Bible Class for the mentally handicapped from different churches can provide support, encouragement and learning at an appropriate level.

Equally important, is that the new member find *a place and a rôle* in the congregation's life. This depends on the level of acceptance and the size of the congregation, but clearly a positive willingness to receive and find a place for the gifts of the so-called handicapped is central to the spiritual-social health of any local Church. Like all such opportunities they arise out of spontaneity and imagination, and cannot be prescribed from outside. This is closely linked with the general need to enable *every* member to exercise his or her gift in the Church's life.

Although our local Monyhull experience is a tentative adaption to people with mental handicap in a particular setting and on the edge of the Church's life, we are convinced that this sacramental experience and the reflection evoked by it brings a profound theological, pastoral and liturgical challenge to the wider Church. The truth is, as Bishop Newbiggin indicates, we are not whole without the handicapped. [24]

NOTES

1. On the general pastoral approach to people with mental handicap: H. W. Stubblefield, *The Church's Ministry in Mental Retardation,* Broadman, 1965; L. Turner, 'The Christian Ministry to the Mentally Handicapped', D. Millard (ed.), *Religion and Medicine,* 3, S.C.M., 1976; B. J. Easter, 'The Bottom of the Barrel or Essential Humanity - ministry and theology in a community for the mentally handicapped', F. Young, G. Wakefield (eds.), *Second City Soundings, Methodist Conference Handbook,* 1985; 'Handicapped, Pastoral Care of (Mentally Handicapped)', A. Campbell (ed.), *Dictionary of Pastoral Care,* S.P.C.K. (forthcoming).

2. There is little descriptive/reflective material on worship with mentally handicapped people, but see: H. W. Stubblefield,

op.cit.; M. Bayley, *The Local Church and Mentally Handicapped People,* C.I.O., 1984; D. Wilson (ed.), *I Am With You,* St Paul, 1975; F. Young, *Face to Face,* Epworth, 1985, pp.80f.; B. J. Easter, 'The Bottom of the Barrel' (sections A and B).

3. On participation and symbolism: D. Wilson, 'Response to Worship', *Emotional Responses of Mentally Handicapped People,* Mencap, S.W. Region Conference, 1983; 'Symbols and Readings', *Liturgy,* 9/5, R.C. Bishops' Conference Liturgy Office, 1985, pp.181-189; J. J. von Allmen, *Worship,* Lutterworth, 1965, pp.93, 240f.

4. For the dramatic view of ritual: V. Turner, *The Ritual Process,* Pelican, 1974; C. Geertz, *The Interpretation of Cultures,* Hutchinson, 1975, pp.448f.

5. For Liturgy as ritual-drama: J. J. von Allmen, *op.cit.,* pp.80f.; S. Winward, *The Reformation of our Worship,* Carey Kingsgate, 1964, pp.53f.

6. J. Calvin, *Institutes of The Christian Religion* (Library of Christian Classics) S.C.M., 1960, IV 14.3.

7. I Corinthians 10: 16-17.

8. Cf. T. F. Torrance, *Theology in Reconstruction,* S.C.M., 1965, pp.26, 70; J. Calvin, *op.cit.,* IV, 14.3.

9. Cf. J. Vanier, *Community and Growth,* Darton, Longman and Todd, 1979, pp.27, 36, 209f.; M. Buber, *The Knowledge of Man,* Allen and Unwin, 1965, pp.72f.

10. Chorus: 'Alleluia', *Sounds of Living Waters,* No.25, cf. R. Anderson, *Historical Transcendence and the Reality of God,* Chapman, 1962, pp.238f.

11. Cf. K. Rahner, 'Dignity of Man', *Theological Investigations* 2, Darton, Longman and Todd, 1963, pp.235f; K. Barth, *Church Dogmatics,* 3/4, T. and T. Clarke, 1969, pp.653f.

12. Cf. V. Turner, *op.cit.,* p.48; F. Dillistone, *Christianity and Symbolism,* Collins, 1955; N. Sagovsky, *Liturgy and Symbolism,* Grove, 1978.

13. C. Geertz, *op.cit.,* pp.448f.; T. F. Torrance, *Theological Science,* Oxford, 1969 pp.196f., 208f.; J. Mcquarrie, *In Search of Humanity,* S.C.M., 1982, pp.68f.

14. *Alternative Service Book* (Rite A); *Book of Common Prayer,*

1662; cf. G. C. Berkouwer, *Conflict with Rome,* Presbyt. and Reformed, 1957, pp.111-112.

15. On embodied apprehension: S. Winward, *op.cit.,* p.69f.; see the profound chapter in J. Calvin, *op.cit.,* IV 17.10.

16. Cf. R. S. Wallace, *Calvin's Doctrine of the Word and Sacrament,* Oliver and Boyd, 1957, pp.218f.; M. Perry, *The Paradox of Worship,* S.P.C.K., 1977, pp.84f.

17. See: J. Calvin, *op.cit.,* IV 14.3.5; 17.42.

18. Cf. *Christian Initiation,* C.I.O., 1971.

19. M. Bayley, *op.cit.,* p.5; H. W. Stubblefield, *op.cit.*

20. See: F. Young, *op.cit.,* pp.75-80; M. Bayley, *op.cit.,* pp.6-8; M. Bayley, *Mental Handicap and Community Care,* Routledge and Kegan Paul, 1973.

21. Cf. H. W. Stubblefield, *op.cit.,* pp.81, 128 on 'feeling tone'.

22. S. Winward, *op.cit.,* p.97.

23. J. Bradford, *Preparing the Mentally Handicapped for Confirmation,* Church of England Children's Society, 1982. Cf. D. Wilson, *I Am With You;* S. Clifford, *Called to Belong,* Kevin Mayhew, 1984; H. R. Hahn, W. H. Raasch, *Helping the Retarded to Know God,* Concordia, 1969.

24. L. Newbiggin, 'Not Whole without the Handicapped', G. Muhler-Fahrenholz (ed.), *Partners in Life,* W.C.C., 1979, pp.17-25.

BRIAN J. EASTER

Mental handicap can appropriately be considered from various standpoints: thus the Church of England tackles it through the Board for Social Responsibility and the United Reformed Church under the Ministry of Healing. For the Baptist Union the fuse was lit when Jill Davis sought educational advice.

The need - but how?

'We're expecting twins!' said Joyce and Jeannette. No, there's no misprint concerning a name, nor was it a fantastic coincidence that two wives in the same church each found themselves about to produce double trouble. Joyce and Jeannette are two remarkable single women, much loved and respected in our fellowship, who foster children - at the time of the above pronouncement, about a baker's dozen! They were preparing us for the fact that Nicholas and Matthew, one year old Down's Syndrome twins, would soon be welcomed into their family.

We were by now used to the long procession of our largest family arrriving en masse and having the immediate effect of filling several rows. And then Nicholas and Matthew came... Two rag-doll-limp, frightened, crying little boys, overwhelmed, as would any child be, at the terrifying change in their everyday world.

I felt an overwhelming sense of responsibility - and panic. It's my job to co-ordinate our children's group work, and questions raced through my mind. Are we ready? How do we communicate to them that they are of infinite value in God's sight? Will they be able to glory in that?

The phone became red hot. Patient friends listened, advised, encouraged. Poor Bryan George, Education Adviser to the Baptist Union, got the lot! A paragraph in the *Baptist Times* brought a startling response: parents, teachers, nurses, church workers, many of them sure the church could do more for the mentally handicapped.

Nicholas and Matthew, just look what you've done!

Thank you, God, for trusting us to care for your children.

JILL DAVIS

At the time Jill's urgent questions about sharing the faith with those babies might have seemed premature, but she could not ignore them. She found she was not alone in her wish to help, nor in her questions about how to go about it. The particular nature of Jill's concern accounts for the Baptist Working Group on Mental Handicap and the Church coming under the auspices of Education. Pastoral and social needs can be approached in terms of educating churches about them. The education 'brief' may, nevertheless, encourage a particular interest in Christian nurture. This section tries to look at what is possible by noting what is being done already, in Sunday School, in preparation for baptism and church membership, in adult classes, and in special services of worship.

GROWING UP IN THE CHURCH

Many of our churches already have a mentally handicapped child in the Sunday School, a mentally handicapped adult in the congregation, or perhaps even in membership. Where one is welcomed, others are often attracted. For some churches it can quickly become a new field of opportunity - or a problem. The church will want to be pastorally supportive. It will also want to make spiritual provision for these people, but how much can they understand?

Some are so profoundly handicapped they are beyond religious understanding as we know it, but many of the handicapped can learn something of God and are capable of very real spiritual life. The state now provides special education as of right. Are the mentally handicapped entitled to a Christian education designed to meet their particular needs? If so, how do we go about it?

Some will get a lot from the children's Sunday School classes, but they cannot stay there indefinitely. Few will cope, in their teens, with deeper Bible study or lively discussion of Christian attitudes to topical issues. We can make special allowances and special provision in order to integrate them, but if teachers 'go overboard' in the effort to include them, that in itself can make it harder for the other children and young people to accept them. A few genuinely find a rôle helping with small children and continue to enjoy the illustrated Bible stories, but that is not a satisfactory answer for many.

Parents know all too well that their child may not fit in easily, and they may need persuading that it is all right to send him. 'When Philip was old enough he was accepted in the primary,' writes one mother. 'I think they must have had the patience of Job to cope with

76

him even for an hour'. (She, of course, coped with him and her other two children all week). Another mother writes of the patience and understanding the teachers showed her daughter; 'It is wonderful to see the Grace of God at work in this need'.

The church service itself is often so verbal and so static, not really visual enough for most of the mentally handicapped. The more charismatic style of service will suit some better, but their tastes vary - just like other people's. I thought my son, brought up in a 'traditional' church, would enjoy the charismatic service when visiting his grandmother. She was startled at his reaction to people who broke into dance - didn't they know how to behave in church? Then some began to talk 'rubbish' - how often he has been told to talk clearly and sensibly! He found it irreverent, where I would have recognised worship, even if not 'my style'. Richard has been more drawn, somewhat to our embarrassment, to 'higher' practices: crossing himself reverently, and even genuflecting as he left our pew to go to Sunday School. However, after a visit to a Russian Orthodox church, we found he drew the line at 'kissing the floor'. It all depends on what you are used to, handicapped or not.

Possibly more significant is that the mentally handicapped may be less obtrusive in churches with livelier patterns of worship, with more movement and interjections from the congregation. Frances Young, a Methodist, observes that she feels more comfortable taking her handicapped and noisy son along when preaching in an independent black church. 'There is no sense there of forcing Arthur on people who would rather not know and cannot cope'. She would hesitate to take him with her when first going to an unfamiliar white congregation. (*Face to Face,* Epworth, 1985)

So while the mentally handicapped will probably enjoy music, drama, puppets, dance, they can also respond positively to an orderly and reverent atmosphere. For many worship is not difficult.

Christian education is much harder. Some hospital chaplains manage a little. At least three Baptist churches run special Bible classes. It can be done. The teaching must be simple and direct, as for children, but the illustrations must not be childish. It is not easy, but it is not impossible.

Unfortunately there is a dearth of suitable material for such classes, or for home use with the adolescent or adult. Bible stories are available at many levels, but not much else, not much to relate the Bible stories to daily life beyond childhood. There is a real need here - but it is not one that appeals to publishers. They doubt whether there is an adequate market. It is encouraging to find one Christian publisher, Christian Publicity Organisation, bringing out study material for poor and non-readers, but even that has limited application for the mentally handicapped. As the leader of the Morningside Bible Class observes, 'I have found there is a great danger of using children's books because they are easy to read and attractive to look at, but these really are not suitable for adults. As a teacher of children with special needs, I am aware that there is a great deal of literature which could be used with them in teaching the Christian faith, but I do not feel that this can automatically be transferred to mentally handicapped adults'.

Christian parents would like to see more churches attempt something in the way of special education. They can feel that it is all left to them. This is something which might usefully be tackled as a joint venture between churches. The need is spelled out in a letter from a mother in Kent: 'We have two little boys who are autistic. They are five and six years and are still in the crèche at the Church. Both are able to understand language, although they say very little, but their anti-social behaviour makes it impossible for them to go into Sunday School... We have prayers together every day with a Bible story and children's hymns and I am sure that in a few years they will understand the Gospel, and hopefully be given Saving Grace to become Christians. Would it be feasible, I wonder, for the Churches to consider holding a Sunday School in a central town, say Canterbury for us, and picking up those mentally handicapped who would benefit by minibus or cars and taking them home again? If it was only once a month it would be useful. Also a simple service for mentally handicapped adults in this way would help these often lonely folk, and give them hope for the future'.

Where churches run social clubs, showing that they care about the handicapped, we might expect them to try to introduce their handicapped friends to Christ. If they do not, it will be because they just do not know where to begin.

Ways need to be found to help the mentally handicapped take a real part in the normal, regular worship of the church. They have little grasp of abstract concepts and so for them, even more than most, it is through His body, the Church, that they are going to encounter Christ. That is why the pastoral care and community action are so important. It is also why the church cannot stop there.

Sometimes the handicapped man or woman can be drawn into the church's midweek study groups. For some it will work well. Elsewhere it may prove difficult. A 'normal' pace will leave them behind, but to proceed at their pace would be limiting for the rest. If they have once been included, is it possible to remove them to a special group without hurting their feelings? There are no rules. The caring church has to work out the right course for itself.

When a church, like Banbury, is such a caring fellowship it

finds it has eight or nine mentally handicapped young people worshipping on Sundays, it has to begin 'to look at ways we can change our worship to reach them, and how to help those teaching them when they go out to their Covenanter classes'.

In the coming years more churches will be in this position. The experience of those who pioneer such work will be well worth sharing.

Three comments sent in by people who have written from their own experience may be helpful:

Mr and Mrs Mayes, whose son has always been made welcome among his own age group in the church, explain, 'For want of a better way to put it, we have treated him as normal, knowing he is handicapped, and for us it has worked'.

Miss Elen Rees, a teacher of handicapped adolescents, writes 'The guideline I tend to use is to halve the age of the person I'm teaching, but to remember because they have lived longer, their experience is wider'.

Mrs Dilys Griffiths, a mother and voluntary worker with the handicapped, observes, 'Any contact with the mentally handicapped must be on their level, no talking down to them, for they understand far more than we realise'.

Much of the teaching considered in these pages is only valid for those handicapped with some understanding of language. Even in a book like this it is difficult not to keep leaving out the profoundly handicapped. The questions remain about whether an 'intellectual' response to the Gospel is necessary for formal inclusion in the church. Nevertheless, a significant proportion of the mentally handicapped are to some extent 'educable', and those who have laboured hard over the years to achieve useful speech, and perhaps some ability to read and write, will like that recognised. Richard, for example, has a good reading vocabulary, but can only sustain reading for short periods. He could never enjoy a novel. He can look up a Bible reference and read two or three verses with understanding – and he delights in that.

FAITH BOWERS

A PLACE IN THE FAMILY OF GOD

Some advice on integrating the handicapped child

It is very hard to write in a general way about children with severe learning difficulties - all children are individual and none more so than the mentally handicapped. Sweeping generalisations are all too common - "All Down's Syndrome children are musical and affectionate" is one of the most popular. It just is not true of many of them. Some have no sense of rhythm and are tone deaf, and if they are all affectionate then some of them have very strange ways of showing it! Down's Syndrome children are an easily recognisable group of children within which there are tremendous variations but there is also a more or less predictable pattern of development. This is not so with brain-damaged children, each of whom has a highly individual and totally unpredictable way of development. It is, therefore, very hard to offer advice on how to cope with these children in church and Sunday School. Each child and each situation is unique, but perhaps the following general guide lines will have some value if applied to the local problem.

1.   Often the most helpful way of integrating a handicapped child into a group is to appoint a 'befriender', one person who will sit with the child at all times, quietly and unobtrusively helping the child along, offering a word of explanation or restraint as necessary, ready to praise and encourage, and prepared to remove the child if the situation is causing too much stress and tension. Someone who has time to give attention to the child, time to build a relationship of trust and acceptance with the child's family and who will not overwhelm the child by making unreasonable demands.

2.   It is important to give the child time to do things for himself. It is instinctive to rush in and help with, for example, putting on coats and doing up buttons, but maybe given time and encouragement he will do it himself and gain a sense of success and achievement. Only do for him the things he truly cannot manage himself.

3.   Speak slowly and clearly, in short, simple sentences, giving one instruction or thought at a time, and breaking tasks down into small, achievable stages. We all like to be successful and it is very important that mentally handicapped children should experience the pleasure of achievement and success.

4.   We must always try to keep the balance, as with all children, between making sufficient demands to stretch and challenge, helping growth and maturity to take place, and creating tension and pressure to such an extent that they either opt out and become

withdrawn or express a sense of failure and inadequacy by showing behaviour problems. Do not worry about how much you are teaching the child. What matters is that he should feel loved and valued for his own sake. Being part of the group is much more important than whether he follows the stories.

5.   As far as possible keep the children within their own peer groups. This should be possible with the help of a befriender. A teenager may have the mental age of a five year old but he has teenage interests and it is usually inappropriate to keep them in the Primary department, even under the guise of 'helper'.

Explain to the other children a little about the mental handicap. To expect them to welcome a 'different' child is asking quite a lot and it is not fair to expect them to 'understand' automatically. Even very young children will respond very differently if they grasp that the mentally handicapped child is not deliberately being silly, but really cannot speak properly, etc. Many will then prove kind, tolerant, and helpful.

6.   Try to assess the particular needs of each child and then find a way of meeting those needs. For example, if the child has a language or communication problem, is he helped by signing? Does he use signing at home or school? It is not too difficult to learn a few basic signs and it could make a tremendous difference to the child (The child's family or school would help with this).

7.   Ask the parents if the child is able to express his own toilet needs, make sure he knows where the toilets are and be prepared to help if necessary. Some mentally handicapped adults may need discreet help with zips and buttons.

8.   Make sure you know whether or not the child has fits and how to cope if it should happen while he is in your care. A fit can look very frightening but may be dealt with simply, making sure the child is safe and offering comfort when it is over. Discuss with the parents the possible signs of a fit coming and how best to cope with their child's pattern of fitting.

9.   Treat the child as normally as possible within their limitations. Expect high standards of behaviour from them, but make sure they know what the boundaries are and what you will accept from them. Instructions need to be clear and firm, even if that may sound more stern than you feel - the child will recognise the difference between a friendly firmness and anger, even if bystanders criticise your strictness. It is important to be consistent and that all the adults have the same standards to which they expect the child to conform. Be sensitive to the child's moods and avoid confrontations. With patience and thought it is usually possible to find a way round

difficulties in such a way that neither child nor teacher loses face.

10. Enjoy the child. Accept and love him as he is, share his pleasures and frustrations. Accept the friendship he has to offer. It is sometimes hard work to build a real relationship with a mentally handicapped child but it is infinitely worthwhile and rewarding to do so. Above all, allow the child to have a measure of self-respect and pride, taking his place in the family of God, loved, valued and accepted as an integral member of the Kingdom.

MARLENE FOX

PHILIP

'He'll have to go!' Heard those words recently from any of your youth leaders, Sunday School teachers or uniformed organisations? We did from time to time over the years, and the subject was sometimes Philip, the Down's Syndrome son of one of our members. Fortunately, the despair would quickly pass. The worst time was when he outgrew his peers and liked to shake a seemingly massive fist in your face. This has now been replaced by equally energetic and enthusiastic hugs.

Philip grew up through the Sunday School, and was accepted into the Boys Brigade. It was marvellous how the boys helped him. He wanted to march like them, be like them, and he tried so hard, even to playing the bugle - but that wasn't a success. Then the Company had a judo class and he was included in that. He loved every minute of it. They helped him in every way to share in the life of the church.

Philip is now twenty-six. He is our most exuberant singer of 'Raise the Cross', his favourite hymn. When his birthday fell on a Sunday he did get the idea that there would be a parade with the band to mark the occasion, but fortunately didn't seem too put out when it didn't materialise. When he became too old for B.B., he was allowed to continue to go to Bible Class and was listened to by the others when he wanted to make a prayer aloud, like the leader.

Before the Union, we were a Churches of Christ congregation and therefore practised Believer's Baptism on confession of faith. We had sometimes discussed what we would do if Philip wanted to be baptised, but never really thinking he would. Well, he did. His faith in the Lord Jesus is beyond doubt. The request for baptism came from him - 'because I love Jesus'. He was insistent, and so he was baptised and has proved to be faithful. He takes a turn as door steward, greeting people and handing out hymn books. He is a regular attender at our communion service.

He had a great desire to read and write and has made some improvement over the years. At Bible Class one January the boys were asked to write what were their hopes for the New Year. When everyone had finished, Philip was still head bent, intent on his labours. What could it possibly be? It was 'Bible, Jesus, baptise'.

It is our custom to have a period of open prayer at the communion service each week, and Philip led a prayer on one occasion to our joy.

If any of you are being driven to distraction at the moment, take heart. The ways of the Lord are indeed mysterious. Who could have thought what a blessing Philip would have proved to his family in the Church? Thanks be to God.

JEAN FORSTER AND EDNA MORGAN

WHAT DOTH HINDER...?

The preceding contribution carries us forward to look at baptismal preparation. As suggested earlier, ministers and churches are not all of one mind over believer's baptism (or, in other denominations, confirmation) for the mentally handicapped. Sometimes they differ because of the way the sacrament is understood, sometimes because of the particular case that has come their way. Most would concede that *some* mentally handicapped people are capable of an adequate profession of faith, and others are quite incapable. But where do you draw the line?

However strict or generous our instincts, we should listen sensitively to thoughtful observations on this:

'Many a mentally handicapped young person has a faith that should put ours to shame. Exclusion from confirmation classes on the grounds that he will not understand will merely emphasise the tendency we have to separate ourselves from those who are not like us'. (Professor Joan Bicknell, senior nurse tutor, writing in *Crucible,* 1983)

'It isn't that we don't want them, but they wouldn't understand about commitment'. (Baptist minister)

'He wished to be baptised... he understood as much as he would ever be able to understand - not the same situation as a child who would wait till he understood more - and so he was baptised'. (Church secretary)

'We must not exploit their susceptibility... Are we really helping them to know God in Christ, or are we only proselytizing in an easy mission field?' (Baptist minister)

'Baptism needs a considerable measure of co-operation on the part of the candidate. I don't see any barrier but ... spectator reaction can be strong in these situations, e.g. finding it cruel, humiliating, unnecessary'. (Baptist minister)

'I find myself being less concerned with signs and more concerned with being a minister of God's grace to those who may receive it'. (Baptist minister)

'It seems to me that the church cannot exemplify the full humanity revealed in Christ, or achieve unity in diversity, if it continues to acquiesce in the social isolation of disabled persons and to deny them full participation in its life'. (Baptist minister)

'The instruction in preparation for Baptism and membership would have to be specially designed, and might not necessarily all precede Baptism. There would in fact be an advantage in post-baptismal nurturing'. (Baptist minister)

The examples that follow are included not to prove that believer's baptism is *always* right for mentally handicapped people - that must be a local individual decision - but rather to show how some churches have gone about it. Having decided baptism was appropriate, they have looked at preparation and ways of making initiation into the church as meaningful as possible. A candidate's conceptual understanding may be minimal or non-existent, his concentration span short, but that does not necessarily mean the he - and the church - do not take baptism seriously.

One minister who baptised a young man with Down's Syndrome a few years ago noted that he had attended the church for a long time with his mother and sister (the latter a church member). He asked his sister about baptism several times over a year or eighteen months, not only when there was a baptismal service. The minister gave elementary instruction, just five minutes a week. Two carefully chosen church members interviewed the candidate, getting a simple response of faith. The church discussed the matter thoroughly, concerned about the extent of his faith. The sister was a helpful witness, knowing what he said and did at home. The church agreed that baptism and membership were appropriate. Friends at a neighbouring church were shocked.

Although a number of ministers have tackled baptismal preparation with a mentally handicapped candidate, it is very hard to establish how they got round the difficulties of working without abstract concepts. Probably because they were never too sure how effective it was, they do not remember details unless actually in the midst of it when asked. One minister suggests a possible way to explain the significance of a symbol would be to work from a handshake, hug or kiss, seeing what they imply and what is offered in return.

This need to find ways round abstractions arises continually. It applies also to talks within a service of worship, as well as to baptismal preparation or group study. The rest of this book is largely concerned with ways this has been done.

ALAN'S BAPTISM

Paddock Road Free Church is a small, basically Baptist, Church serving a small area often called 'Oxhey Village' within the Watford/Bushey district. Alan Brown, at 23, is the eldest child in one of the Church families, his mother being a very active member. Alan suffers from a fair degree of both physical and mental handicap though neither prevent him from living a fairly independent life, residing in a community home for mentally handicapped in Stevenage. His parents live opposite a MENCAP residential home for girls and both are heavily involved in its work. Most of the girls, some of whom are very severely handicapped, worship regularly at the Church on Sunday evenings.

Almost twelve months ago Alan indicated that he had made a decision for Christ and that he wished to be baptized. The matter was carefully considered by the Church Executive, including his mother, most of whom had known him all his life. While the final decision was left to myself as the 'Church Superintendent', the Executive was unanimous that Alan should be baptized, in recognition of the fact that he understood the meaning of his decision as fully as he would ever do and in the light of his undoubted sincerity.

The baptismal preparation was undoubtedly extremely important - perhaps more so even than normal, though it obviously had to be tailor-made for Alan. The one-to-one classes took place in Alan's home on Sunday afternoons, and while covering the usual range of subjects, i.e. conversion, baptism, Church membership, Communion,

Witness, missionary interest, followed the pattern of my providing written notes for Alan to study during the week for us then to discuss together the following week. In this way I was not presenting Alan with ideas which were completely new to him. We also used Stephen Winward's *New Testament teaching on Baptism* as daily readings over the period, which Alan happily used in conjunction with a beautiful new Bible which Alan's parents had given him to mark the occasion. The whole series lasted two months and towards the end concentrated on the actual baptismal Service. Alan himself chose the music on a visit to his uncle who was going to be the organist at the Service.

The character of that Service was in many ways very different from normal. The whole atmosphere was that of a birthday celebration. Specially printed cards were used, inviting relatives, friends, neighbours etc. to Alan's Baptism, and indeed the small building, which seats some 80 and normally has an evening congregation of 20-30, was filled. During the Service, because of a fairly marked speech difficulty, Alan was only asked to make a simple response to a set of confessional questions, rather than give a testimony. The Evening Service is normally followed by tea and biscuits. On this occasion it was followed by a birthday party - to celebrate Alan's new birth. One friend had made a beautifully iced cake in the form of an open Bible and many members of the congregation gave Alan a small present. The end result was a Service which was very meaningful for Alan, and very moving for those who know and love him.

It was also unanimously agreed that Alan should enter into full Church membership, since it was felt that membership signified not the right to attend and ability to contribute to Church business meetings but acceptance by and entry into the Body of Christ.

JIM CLARKE

STEPHEN'S BAPTISM

'I want to be baptized'. I wonder how many people with mental handicap have either said or somehow communicated this desire, and how many times this request may have been over-ruled on the basis that there was insufficient understanding, or means of expressing faith.

Stephen had always attended Church with us from the time he was born, he had been in Crèche, Beginners, Primary, moving on into Juniors later than normal (chronologically) but taking his part as far as possible in all the activities. He had joined the Boys Brigade rather late, as a teenager, and carried out badge work to the best of his ability. He had joined the Band, playing the cymbals and occasionally a tenor drum, with a tremendous sense of rhythm and he took part in all the displays, showing quite an aptitude for drill.

We had long observed Stephen's sense of worship and whilst not really being able to talk about faith (although he is very articulate) we felt he had a real awareness of Jesus. He had been present at his sister Debbie's baptism when she was 13, and his brother Jonathan's at 18. Now he was 18 and feeling very positive that he should take this step.

Our minister, the Revd Alan Griggs, felt very happy to include Stephen in the next Baptismal Preparation Group (on this occasion all fairly young candidates). We know that Stephen may not have expressed his faith during this time in ways that would normally have been expected but Alan had no hesitation in agreeing to his Baptism.

Stephen attends an Adult Training Centre and in the week leading up to his Baptism he sat for a total of six hours and painstakingly wrote to every Instructor in the Centre inviting them to the service. Alan announced at the morning service that tissues would be given out with the hymn books that night! It is true to say that many people, not the least Stephen's own family, had tears in their eyes as Stephen entered the waters of Baptism that night, and we heard Alan say that he felt it a privilege to baptize him in the Lord's name. His face was radiant as he came up out of the water and said for all to hear 'I did it - I've been baptized'. And what a witness it was, as every one of his Instructors, most of them non-Christians, had responded to his invitation and attended the service - all of them deeply moved by the experience.

It was some while before Stephen asked for Church membership. He was interviewed in the usual way, and I'm sure the interviewers found it a slightly unusual chat. However, they wholeheartedly recommended him for membership. His actions, they said, had already indicated how loyally he could serve his Church. He has now been a Sidesman for about a year. He takes his duties very seriously, never misses a duty unless it is unavoidable, and on those occasions arranges his own substitute. He always has a welcoming smile and handshake as he greets people at the door, efficiently takes up the offering and clears books away after the service. He rarely misses a service or Church Meeting and many people say he cheers them by his presence.

How we thank God that we have had the joy of seeing all three of our children commit their lives to the Lord. It seems impossible that once we were told by a well meaning and kindly doctor that our youngest child would never be able to do anything and so we might as well put him away and forget we ever had him. What a tremendous experience we would have missed if we had taken his advice. It hasn't always been easy, but we have always known that God had a purpose in sending us this very special child and with his child-like faith he has committed his life to the Lord's service. Jesus said 'Anyone who refuses to come to God as a little child will never be allowed into His Kingdom'.

BARBARA CROWE

EXPLORING TOGETHER

Following a baptismal service when several young people were baptized, Richard asked for baptism. He had said, several years earlier, that one day he wanted to 'get into the water with Barbara' - but this was different. Over the last year Richard had begun to stay in church for communion services and sometimes shared the act of communion. He has been a steward at church services and taken up the offertory; he is involved in the preparation and serving of lunch in the Friendship Centre. Richard had begun to share more fully in the life of the Church in an adult and responsible way.

Richard is a Down's Syndrome child of 16. When I tried to probe why he wanted to be baptised, he said 'I love Jesus'. As far as I am concerned, this response is enough. I have been responsible for trying to help young people in baptismal classes for some years. I see the response of faith as a miracle of grace, coming to people in a myriad different ways. Some young people, even very bright ones academically, find it difficult to be articulate about the growing faith within them.

Richard and I now have weekly sessions together when we try to discover more about Jesus, the Church and being a Christian. Throughout his Sunday School days Richard has always been in a class with other children, usually children younger in age than himself. Whilst he is accepted by the other children, it is becoming increasingly obvious to Richard that he is older than the group with whom he has associated through the years and yet is out of his depth in discussions with sixteen year olds who are into boy friends, O levels etc. So these private sessions are enjoyed by Richard and I find I can also enjoy him without the added pressure of divided concerns. He still meets with the other young people in the Sunday School class, so these private sessions are extra and do not separate him off from the others.

I discussed with his parents the need for visual material. His mother produced a very helpful file, to which we constantly refer, with sections:

1. About Jesus: This tells simply of the life of Jesus, his birth, teaching, healing ministries, the trial, cross and resurrection, the work of the Holy Spirit in our lives. This is all illustrated with pictures from Christmas cards, postcards etc. and some of the pictures were drawn and Richard coloured. The script is in simple sentences which Richard can read easily and the pages on the work of the Holy Spirit have some illustrations from Richard's own experience of life.

2. The Church: The illustrations here are photographs of our own Church - 'a place where Jesus' friends meet to worship God, together'. One or two of the photographs Richard took himself. There are pictures of the building, the congregation at worship, the minister preaching, the organist. There are also pictures of people serving within the church - a lady arranging flowers, stewards, maintenance and cleaning, meals served in the Centre. Richard has always felt 'at home' in the fellowship of the Church and the pictures speak of a fellowship of people whom he knows are all 'his friends'.

3. Baptism: Photos were taken of a recent baptismal service - the preparation for the baptism, and the baptisms. Richard has copied from the Bible the story of Jesus' baptism. He knows that 'People are baptised to show they love Jesus'.

4. Communion: This section begins with an artist's impression of the Last Supper - with the link that Jesus told his friends to take bread and wine to help them think about him. Again there are pictures of a communion service at Bloomsbury, minister and deacons serving and people being received into membership.

Our weekly sessions together are quite short. Richard's concentration wanes after 20 minutes or so. I envisage the 'course' taking about a year. Each week we look at and read the Bible together, using the Good News Bible. The GNB is helpful in these sessions, particularly with the illustrations to hand, but confuse Richard when he tries to follow the reading in Church where a different version is often used.

Apart from reading together, we write and illustrate our theme.

I take one concept per week and try to use language and draw from experiences which will be meaningful. Sometimes I grope blindly because abstract words and concepts are incomprehensible for him. So far we have looked together at the themes

God the Creator of the universe - using the Bible and also the hymn 'God who made the earth' - illustrating with pictures which Richard chose and assembled.

Who is Jesus Christ? - again using the Bible and the prepared folder, illustrating one main point - Jesus as the Son of God.

Prayer - We have had at least five sessions on prayer. One week we looked at the prayer Jesus taught his friends, and Richard copied out the Lord's Prayer for 'homework'. He likes homework - it provides a link with other children who have homework; his special school does not set homework. Then we divided prayer into four sessions and each week I encouraged Richard to make his own prayers. Later I wrote down his thoughts and he copied them as homework in his own prayer book.

We looked at prayer as 'Thank you' prayers - and his own prayers included rhubarb crumble and thick custard! Sorry prayers were more difficult - a few promptings from parents on events in the previous week helped. We then looked at Help prayers - for self and for others. Prayers for self included asking God to help him at school to try hard with reading, writing and maths. Prayer for others involved looking at the newspaper and cutting out pictures of people who needed our prayers. We talked about the events which the pictures illustrated and the needs of people and then I encouraged Richard to give his own words for a prayer. 'Dear God, we know you love people. Please help people who get hurt, sometimes rough men hurt others. On TV we see that people get killed and their families are very sad. Please help doctors and nurses and help all sad people'. We cut out pictures to illustrate the prayer.

We have begun to look at Communion. We think of it as a friendship meal - Richard understands about friends. Jesus shared with his friends and told us to share together, remembering and saying thank you to him.

I am thinking that a way in for Baptism may well be through planting seeds - buried in the soil - growing new plants.

We are still exploring together. I learn constantly to watch the language I use in any conversation - there has to be a grappling to find a 'way in' through an idea Richard can grasp. Abstract concepts are impossible. There are many rewards in our exploration together. There is a simplicity and directness about Richard's faith which is salutary and cleansing. I am grateful for the opportunity of helping Richard recognise, accept and fulfil his true destiny as a child of God.

BARBARA STANFORD

The next three contributors are all involved in general Christian nurture of the mentally handicapped. A barrister, a secondary school teacher, and a minister, all brought voluntarily into this special ministry through their commitment to Christ, they have had to explore new lines of communication.

"CAN SAY A PRAYER, YOU KNOW"

"Everywhere. Not see him. Talk to him".

Each week John makes his statement of faith and adds, "Can say a prayer, you know". Sometimes he says it in a traffic jam on the A40 and as often as not he will then add "Traffic lights. Amen", indicating his analysis of why we are going to be late for church again and what God ought to do about it.

John is on his way to the Stone Sunday Club at Haven Green Baptist Church in West London. There he will meet up with Mary and Susan, and perhaps Anne and Peter, as he has been doing for ten years. He is one of the original members of the Stone Club. The Club itself was started by Roger Chapman, a social worker who was a member of the Church. He knew that God loved mentally handicapped adults but sensed that God's Church did not always show that in a way such adults could understand. So he started the club and named it after the stone that rolled away from the mouth of the tomb to let the Risen Jesus be seen by the world.

Roger led the club for several years and trained other church members in the work. At its largest the club had about twenty members, four of whom were helpers from the church and the rest members from local authority hostels, group homes and training centres. Today the club has a leader and three regular members, John, Mary and Susan. That is about the right ratio. With more leaders, the club could take more members.

On a Sunday the club members share in the worship of the whole congregation for a while and then they leave to continue in their own meeting. Sometimes that is held in the church kitchen over coffee; sometimes it is held on a bench in a local park - because God is everywhere, although you can't see him, and you can talk to him and say a prayer even though you are not in church.

Because God is very interested in everyone, the meeting begins with an exchange of news: that gives club members a chance to start a conversation about things that are important to them, rather than simply reacting to, or being overwhelmed by, talk directed by people who have less difficulty in conversing.

Then Mary writes down three headings - "Thanking Prayers", "Asking Prayers", and "Praising Prayers", and under each heading is put down a topic chosen by each member from the news they have shared. The list is then read over, and it is time to talk to God.

"Pray to God. I'm glad people are coming to my house to tea. Amen", says the sociable Susan.

"Auntie. Amen", says John, and in that one word thanks God for the lady who looks after him and asks God to bless her.

Then Mary prays a longer prayer, complete with lines from choruses and verses of Scripture.

Singing, unaccompanied or to a tape, plays a large part, and there is no greater delight than a visitor coming with a guitar.

And then it's learning time - "learning" rather than "teaching" because it is hard to say who is teaching whom. The assumption that the group leader is doing the teaching is not always borne out by events.

Those who work with mentally handicapped adults soon learn the value of spontaneity, unreserved affection and the lack of any barrier between thinking and doing, and quickly appreciate the heavy emphasis in Baptist churches upon the sung or spoken word, which may not be heard or understood by many, and which deprives them of full participation in the worship of the community. If God is the friend who made Coca Cola and flowers and sunshine and is with us all the time and wants us to talk to him, then we say "Thank you, God" - out loud, in the middle of the cafe, and to the evident embarrassment of those who spend their Sunday mornings differently. And just in case they didn't hear first time, we shout "Amen".

If they don't come to church, the Stone Club takes the Church to them. How's that for a lesson? And in giving it, the members of the Stone Club are less handicapped than you or me.

ALASTAIR NORRIS

LIFEWAY BIBLE CLASS

As the children leave the hall of Stirling Baptist Church after their morning session, the 25 to 30 members of the next Bible Class are waiting on the doorstep. Nine or ten will have been to morning worship at the Baptist church next door, five more will have worshipped in their own churches (Church of Scotland, Roman Catholic), but most are collected from their homes in the social work minibus. The bus is provided free, and driven by a rota of church folk with 'escorts' drawn from the young people, a number of them University students. The class meets for an hour, 12.30 to 1.30, from September to the end of June. The home run afterwards takes a further 45 minutes.

The Lifeway Bible Class is for mentally handicapped adults (aged 16 to mid-50s). The range of handicap is wide. Several have other disabilities too: blindness, deafness, epilepsy. Some lack the power of speech. All are, however, mobile to greater or lesser degrees. Most attend the same day centre during the week. One has a job, as a road sweeper.

The class has been running for twenty years. It began when a church member was concerned about the lack of suitable teaching for her Down's Syndrome daughter once she was over Sunday School age. There is a need for simple adult teaching. It can be difficult for the mentally handicapped to integrate in the normal adult Bible studies, which they cannot follow. Their understanding may be that of a child, but they do paid work at an Adult Training Centre all week, they watch adult TV and films, and they are rightly sensitive to anything that might suggest they were being treated like children. This can lead to problems even in this special class, for some would enjoy art and craft work, while others would be deeply offended at the suggestion. It is almost impossible to convince them that adults do craft! To offer different options – to let some paint while others study William Barclay's commentaries – has proved difficult with present time and resources.

The aims of the class are:

1. to provide an atmosphere where each member can become more aware of Jesus and His claims on their lives

2. to give biblical teaching applied to daily life in an intelligible form

3. to treat each member as *adult* and expect participation and behaviour as near 'normal' as possible

4. to integrate members into other church activities as and when possible, e.g. services, fellowship weekends, coffee rotas etc.

A typical class pattern would be:

> Opening hymn
> Praise
> Revise previous week's teaching (oral questions and answers), plus first teaching block 10-15 minutes
> Offering
> Prayer time: intercession
> Hymn/Chorus
> Second teaching block, with visual aids 10-15 minutes
> Prayer: petition
> Hymn
> Benediction (all join in the Grace)

Music is very popular - it has to be limited or nothing else would be done. Tapes are used in teaching when possible. Choruses to a guitar are especially enjoyed. MIND hymnbooks were used, but when they dropped to bits we felt a need for a larger number of hymns and choruses and now use our own selection, *Praise Jesus* and *Jesus Praise*. The class tends to be very conservative, and would stick entirely to hymns they have been singing for years, but new ones are introduced slowly, until they become familiar. Recently a wide range of *Jesus Praise* choruses have become popular and accepted.

Some members have been in the class from the beginning, and this can lead to complications. The original small group is well acquainted with most Bible stories, whereas newcomers may have no Bible knowledge at all. Sometimes it is possible to split into two groups for study, the older ones talking about what the Bible teaches about some aspect of Christian living, while the younger ones do basic Bible study. The balance must also be kept between being very simple and yet adult enough for the more able. Many can read a little, and in a small group we can read the Good News version for ourselves. About three quarters of the members have their own faith in Christ.

General course books have been a problem. 'Primary' books are too elementary and 'Bible Class' books a bit too abstract. We used the Salvation Army series *Living and Believing* until they were discontinued. They included material for various levels, and with forethought and adaptation we found them good. We now use some Scripture Union 10-14s courses adapted. We prepare some courses ourselves, with folders and practical work, e.g. on Mark's gospel, St Paul, Prayer. We try to balance Old and New Testament teaching, and to combine biblical teaching with contemporary references. We try to talk about modern Christians as much as we can: we have used *The Hiding Place, Mister Leprosy* and *Joni* with profit.

We encourage as many members as can to take part (it is easier to do it oneself, but this has to be resisted!). Prayers, Bible readings, etc. are all done by members at various times.

Three helpers share the teaching, with four more who help to lead singing, prayers, group work, and teach one week in six or seven. Student friends have served faithfully through essay crises and exams, and are very popular with the class. There is always sadness when they graduate and move on. We have recently increased the number of helpers - the more the better, we find, for finding places in bibles, talking about concerns and worries. Shy adults find the class a 'non-threatening' place to be where they are totally accepted.

Each autumn we collect for a Tear Fund project, sending about £100 each Christmas. The excellent posters and project sheets are very popular. We also have links with missionaries in Pakistan, Indonesia and Kenya, and send them gifts. Other money goes go to the local hospice, etc. We try to encourage weekly stewardship: the tendency can be to drop whatever pence you find in your pocket in the collection.

We keep the role of the class under close review, being well aware that integration of the handicapped is important. The members are very enthusiastic about the class and want it as a separate entity, but we try to have as many integrated occasions as we can.

Some attend the morning service regularly, and a few have been baptised and are full church members. They sometimes come to midweek Bible studies and join in coffee rotas etc. It can be difficult as they are keen to help and some discretion is needed. Some are *desperate* to sing in the choir, but are tone deaf. Others would like to help in the creche, but frighten small children. Problems can arise in the service, especially if the minister asks rhetorical questions! Some want to sit right at the front and are unpredictable. Most church members are tolerant.

We encourage links with the young people, but none of the handicapped want to go to the Young People's Fellowship.

Twice a year we have residential weekends when about ten of the handicapped and ten helpers (class staff, their families, young people) go to the Atholl Baptist Centre at Pitlochry, which is equipped for the handicapped. Then there is little feeling of 'them' and 'us'. We all share domestic tasks, table tennis, outings, and Bible studies. This is hard work, but a great help in deepening fellowship. As our own kindness, patience, tolerance and love are tested, we begin to understand something of the strain families live under when one member needs constant help. Some of the class members had never been away before - for their parents it was the first break in twenty years. Quite 'ordinary' things can present such difficulty. On one occasion we did not realise one girl could not recognise her own clothes. Nobody knew she was dressed in two layers of everything while we all searched high and low for the missing garments!

We have a summer outing, sometimes with the Sunday School though they tend to arrange activities for the very physically active, which do not really suit our members. Often we invite parents and elderly friends, and encourage the class members to look after their guests. Some find it very hard to offer food round before eating themselves!

The Christmas party is the most integrated event of the year. About seventy class members, friends, brothers and sisters, all mix together for food, games, Scottish and disco dancing. On that evening noone really knows or thinks about who is handicapped or not.

The rewards of working with this class are many. They have a deep concern for anyone in trouble: they always supply a long list of people for whom intercession is asked. Compared with working in a secondary school, they are pure *joy* to teach. Their patience with those who try to teach is touching. In school you are alert for trouble if, for example, you drop a book. This class simply tells you not to worry and waits till you are ready. Once we were trying to illustrate possible results of quarrels and one of us, deliberately, knocked over a jar of water. The point was lost as there was a mad rush to the door for a cloth. They are usually eager to help. They have little sense of feeling sorry for themselves: they all know people worse off and count their blessings. Their faith is real, and it is a privilege to hear some of them pray.

There are some difficulties. All week they work at the same training centre and tensions there can spill over to Sundays. We have had one or two fights with the younger ones. It is very difficult to convince them that 'an eye for an eye' is not the best way to live. Some can feel superior because they come to Bible Class, and so antagonise others - we are all human!

The opportunities for home visitation are endless. We are always well received, and are often the only Christian link. Many parents have health problems themselves, most are old and deeply worried about the future of their sons and daughters. Visits are often requested. The class leader is often the only visitor at time of sickness. She tries to share a word from the Bible and a prayer in each home. Homes are often very crowded. The welcome is usually warm and humbling. There are many opportunities for evangelism.

To anyone who might start a class for the mentally handicapped, we would give great encouragement. We certainly do not know all the answers in sharing the gospel with these friends. We learn by trial and error. We have to be flexible, humble, patient. We may express things in too complicated a way, or we may state the obvious – but they are very patient with us. It is a privilege to work with them.

THE 'LESSON' - SOME ADVICE AND A SAMPLE

A teacher's advice

1. It is important to start with something everyone can join in – there is so easily a 'sleeping' section of the class.

2. I like to start a teaching section of 10-15 minutes with short questions and answers and build up to the main point. Then break for offering/hymn/prayer, then resume the teaching. The pace has to be built up again – you cannot just go on where you left off.

3. Content needs to be simple, but delivered with a great variety of pace and verbal emphasis.

4. Beware of having too much material. The longer I teach, the less material I have – but reinforce it more strongly.

5. Include lots of references to their daily life: work at the Training Centre, social life, TV etc.

6. Any humour in illustrations is greatly appreciated. Often they see jokes I haven't noticed myself.

7. 'Drama' goes down well, either performed by staff or using class members. It must be kept short and to the point, and not allowed to get BORING.

A sample lesson

This lesson was based on 'God Speaks: 4. Jesus the Word' from Learning Together with 11-14s, Scripture Union, October-December 1984.

After opening praise and prayer I held up a Concise Oxford Dictionary.

Eileen (with enthusiasm):   Who knows what this is?
Jardine: A Dictionary.
Eileen: And what would we find inside it?
Chorus: Words.
Eileen: Yes. Do you like words? *(6 out of 25 say they do)* I do, very much. The longest word in English used to be 'antidisestablishmentarianism' - I used to like saying that and then I discovered that I married someone who wrote books about it. *(Much laughter!)*
Now I want you to think hard. What do we use words <u>for</u>?
(Long pause)   Any offers?
Jim: So that if someone wants information they can get it.
Eileen: Yes, very good. If you ask someone the way, it's useful if they can <u>tell</u> you it. It's not the only way, of course.
Jardine (breaks in):   No, you can use signs as well.
Robert: And maps.
Eileen: Very true, but words are useful. Do you all agree?
(Give time for all to agree - it wakes up the sleepers!)
Eileen: I want you to look at this little scene. We are at a bus stop in Stirling.
(Very simple acting, by two staff)
Eileen: Excuse me, do you know if the Bridge of Allan bus has gone yet?
Mary (crossly): How should I know? I'm catching the Alloa bus so I'm not looking for the Bridge of Allan bus.

Eileen: Excuse me, do you know if the Bridge of Allan bus has gone yet?
Mary: Now, I'm not sure - I don't think it has and you could always change in the town centre - you'd get there quicker that way.

Eileen: Excuse me, do you know if the Bridge of Allan bus has gone yet?
Mary: I don't know. You can never tell these days, the buses never run on time and they are always on strike.

Eileen: Right, how did Mrs Allen change during those interviews?

(It took some time to sort out that she was cross, helpful, and then complaining)
So, it was what she said that showed us what sort of person she was.
Chorus: Yes.

Eileen: I want you to turn now to p.118 in your Bibles.
(Pause for all to find, even if they cannot read).

"In the beginning was the Word". That's very odd, isn't it? What on earth does that mean?
(Blank looks – even from those in the class 17 years)
Well, who was God's Word in John's Gospel?
Jardine: God .
Eileen: Not really.
George: The Spirit.
Eileen: Not really.
Gina: Jesus.
Eileen: Yes. Why did John call him the Word?
Well, we believe God spoke in lots of different ways. For example, he 'spoke' and the world was created. You talked about him speaking to Jeremiah two weeks ago and then giving messages through angels to Mary and Elizabeth *(lesson last week)*. Well, when he sent Jesus, this was his clearest message ever, so Jesus is called The Word.

In Jesus we can see what God himself is like. What sort of person was Jesus?
Various: Loving, kind, obedient, holy, cross at wrong, etc. etc.
Eileen: We can see that God is like that through what Jesus did and said. God is loving, kind, holy...
Jim: Yes, he would have been a Conservative.
(This is the sort of remark that throws one and leaves one speechless at its appalling implications!)
Eileen: So, Jesus shows us what God is like.

(Offering at this point and we sing 'Jesus Name above all Names')

Eileen (holding up an invitation): This is an invitation. How many of you have had invitations to parties over Christmas?
(Many hands go up. We spend a few moments discussing who is going to which discos etc – a general interest raiser)
Eileen: I'm going to a party on Friday. This is my invitation. Can you see at the bottom of it it has R.S.V.P. Do you know what that means?
(Very blank looks)
Gina (eventually, the only one who knows): It means you have to reply.
Eileen: Yes, absolutely right. *(More talk about R.S.V.P.)*
And it's as if Jesus has R.S.V.P. on him from God. God didn't just send Jesus to do all those good things long ago. What happened to Jesus? *(Quick questions and answers)*
 - He was born in Bethlehem. Yes.
 - He died and rose again.
Eileen: And we have to reply or respond. God said 'I love you enough to send my Son to you to die for you'. What's your reply?
(Pause) How can we reply?
Janine: Talk to him back.
Eileen: Yes. We call that Prayer.
Robert: Help other people.

Eileen: Yes, as Jesus did.
Jim: Read the Bible.
Eileen: Yes.
(Beware of pious phrases thcy think will please you!)
Eileen: We can trust him, can't we? We can say we are sorry for the wrong things we do and ask him to help us every day to live a good life. *(General agreement).*
So it's Christmas next week. When you think of baby Jesus, think of what he can mean to you today, and reply to God's Word.

(Hymn, prayer, choruses)

[This lesson was more direct on response than some as it was the last in a series leading up to Christmas. The Jeremiah lesson, for example, had a quite different emphasis. The time taken for this was about 35–40 minutes]

EILEEN M. BEBBINGTON

GAMES WITH CHRISTIAN APPLICATION

The Revd Gerald Forse of Chipping Norton Baptist Church ministers to a local home. He uses games to help the residents become familiar with some Christian themes.

PICTURE LOTTO with a Christian application

The adult residents of the mentally handicapped unit were familiar with a simple PICTURE LOTTO table game. Christian motifs were substituted.

A set of 12 boards were prepared from coloured thin card measuring $10\frac{1}{2}$ x $10\frac{1}{2}$ ins. and 48 cards at $5\frac{1}{8}$ x $5\frac{1}{8}$ ins. Each large card featured four motifs, in different combinations of designs, and the small cards had corresponding motifs, each of twelve designs appearing four times. It was possible to have double-sided games. One featured the Christmas carol 'Away in a manger', with motifs such as a stable, the manger, the stars, a child, a cow, etc. The reverse featured the motifs of the 'Butterfly Song', with the addition of 'Mr Men' to make up the number. The cards were covered with clear Fablon to make them more durable.

The twelve players, seated at a table, have to match the small cards as they are called to the designs on the larger boards, which are distributed among them.

The motifs need to be fairly basic, but experience has shown that many of the residents are able to 'achieve'. Also they tend to help each other.

Another set was prepared in the same way as the first, except that this time motifs were associated with numbers. One (lost) sheep, Two hands (in prayer), Three gifts (from the wise men), Four seeds (from the parable of the sower), etc. In this case the small cards had the motif, a number (1 to 12), and a word ('Sheep', etc.). On one side of the large cards were the motifs only and on the other the numbers only. Two possibilities were then open, either matching the motifs, or matching the numbers. The residents seemed to cope equally well with both. The extra material on the small cards did not seem to confuse, and the numbers were identified equally well as before. Some residents obviously could not identify motifs or numbers, but a significant number could participate.

Another use for the small cards has been to issue each of twelve residents with one out of the set of four designs and then place the remainder on chairs etc. around the room, and then set them to collect the others in the set. The same kind of capability can be observed.

This has been a small attempt to adapt games with which the residents are familiar to a Christian emphasis. The basic technique needs to be linked with simple adult teaching.

GERALD FORSE

O WORSHIP THE LORD

'Those we call mentally handicapped are capable of a life of faith...
They are capable of coming close to God, and of even surprising us
by the way they can live the gospel in their daily lives. It means,
however, that we must get to know them well, as close friends, and
not as teachers. It also means that we listen to them and see them
with the eyes and ears of faith. It is only our faith which gives
value to the soft-spoken phrases, and to the clumsy gestures which
another cannot see, but which are the expression of a handicapped
person's belief in the God who lives with him and in him'.

The most moving recent affirmations about the spiritual life
possible in the mentally handicapped are made in a Roman Catholic
introduction to religious special education (*I am with you,* ed. David
G. Wilson, St Paul Publications, 1975). Some of the Catholic details
may fall awkwardly on Baptist ears, but this is an exciting and
challenging book for any Christian concerned with the mentally
handicapped.

One of the examples given of those clumsy expressions of faith
rang particularly true to me, for I have seen my own son react
similarly. Peter's catechist had talked to him gently about suffering,
and the sufferings of Jesus. A week later television news showed the
injured in a rail crash. Peter pointed, saying repeatedly, 'Jesus,
cross'. Richard has also associated the cross with mass suffering
depicted in the news. Less grimly, when a loved uncle died and we
told Richard he had gone to be with Jesus, Richard stretched his
arms out sideways and asked if he had died like Jesus. Although
assured the uncle was not crucified but died gently, Richard years
later will still stretch out his arms when he speaks of that uncle who
was close to Jesus and who died.

'When we talk about the use of the intellect, we refer as a rule
to the ability to reason... the intuitive way that the intellect works
can be overlooked. Intuition enables a person to learn and to know
by means of a sort of sympathy... something like that obscure
process whereby a lover comes to know his beloved, or whereby we
are strongly yet inarticulately grasped by a beautiful piece of music,
or a beautiful sunset... With the mentally handicapped it may be the
only faculty of the intellect to be truly active'.

My friend's eight year old son looked at her plants of various
shapes and sizes, arrayed on the window sill. 'Look, a crib!' 'A
crib?' asked his mother, puzzled. Christmas was long past. 'Yes,'
said David, 'There's Jesus in the manger, that one's Joseph, Mary,
shepherds...' And mother's eye had only seen foliage there!

I once showed David, whose family are Anglicans, a Children's Communion Book, The front cover shows an urban scene and then, in the foreground, communicants at the altar without church walls separating them from the 'world'. David studied this and was puzzled. Eventually, slowly, he pronounced, 'There's no bell'. At his church the bell summons people to worship, and then is struck solemnly twice to mark the taking of the bread and wine. David's parents are not particularly keen on such 'high' practice, but David likes the bell and listens for it. For him it has a significant part in worship. So the absent walls did not bother him, but he missed the bell.

They may not think along the same channels as the rest of us, but such intuitive connections may surprise us. They may show how real to them is what they know of religion - like the time my son saw the sign STABLE beside Epsom race course and thought he might find Mary and Joseph there. We may chuckle - but occasionally their unexpected response can make us pause for thought.

'The mentally handicapped are remarkably sensitive in their relationships with others. They will quickly detect what is not authentic about us'. David Wilson goes on to point out that this will apply also to what they see of our devotions. Reverence and prayerfulness will be noticed. Similarly they may 'feel' for what is good or bad, without necessarily understanding why.

'In many activities of family life it can be difficult to include the handicapped child, or he lags behind. But in the service and love of God the unity of the family can be complete - all are equal'.

David Wilson's section on prayer is also helpful.

'The mentally handicapped child starts to pray, as every other child does, in the cradle. Prayer is entering into God's presence. It is the prayer of the parents that carries the child they love with them to the Father. Over the years the child associates a special quietness, a tone of voice, his own hands being put together, with something that means a great deal to his parents. Everything in the family which leads to the recognition of God's presence helps the child to pray'.

'The prayer of praise comes naturally to most mentally handicapped children. They are capable of wonder'. This can be expressed in gesture: stretching the arms out, clapping and dancing with joy, or pausing in silent rapture. 'A mentally handicapped child is often completely at home with the prayer of quiet, provided he is guided to it and encouraged'.

This praise can be brought, with thanksgiving, into home life and family prayer. Here celebration of special events in family life and in the church calendar, leads on into other forms of prayer.

When the book moves on to prayer at church, showing the value to the handicapped of liturgy and symbols, Baptists may feel uneasy. Does our puritanical rejection of so much of this make life harder for our handicapped sons and daughters? Yet even here the Catholics still have a relevant and encouraging word for us: 'He will participate before he understands. His way of participating will be his own response. We should not be put off by the clumsy actions, the discordant singing, the time lag in the responses. In all this it is God who is being glorified'.

Thus we move into the church service. 'Parents are often worried if their child will not sit still, or remain silent, or attend to what is happening. It is impossible to be dogmatic here. There are degrees of disturbance. Perhaps it is more important for the parents to make sure their attitude is correct, than to be always checking and scolding their youngster beside them... We don't go for a few moments of quiet prayer, but for being together in worship'.

It is easier said than done, isn't it? Those ever sensitive parents of the handicapped are easily embarrassed. They will hear acutely every murmur and scuffle. They need encouragement from friends and help in judging what is acceptable and when the distraction is too great for others. Whether their neighbours pointedly ignore or turn with scowl or smile sympathetically will affect their will to return.

Turning to the experience in our Baptist churches and to older handicapped worshippers, it is clear that helping in practical ways can be valuable in involving them in worship. 'Who sweeps a room as for Thy cause...'. The little tasks, like changing the preacher's water, putting up hymn numbers, tidying the pews, can all be important. Some are able and delighted to take their turn as stewards, welcoming people, handing out hymnbooks, taking up the offering. The old deacon who has long supervised our communion arrangements is in hospital; but I could hear her voice when my son lectured me on how to collect up the glasses without chipping them!

The difficult verbal parts of the service are much more tolerable when you know you have a contribution to make within the context of communal worship. 'Belonging' is part of worship, and a splendid antidote to boredom. Being entrusted with jobs for the church is one sign of belonging, and it figures repeatedly in the letters we have received.

The handicapped are often more positive about this belonging than many other worshippers. The sermon does not necessarily pass over their heads. Ministers are often startled to receive answers to their rhetorical questions!

When handicapped adults come to worship together, not with families and not necessarily with a Christian upbringing behind them, the church may need to work out how best to help, and possibly control, them. Will they sit apart? They often like front pews whence they can see better. Is it more welcoming - or officious - to join them? Mr Astill, pastor at Ash Street, Bootle, suggests a caring mean: 'In services they sit together, and any help that they may occasionally require is given by other members who sit close by, but not next to our Mencap friends. We seek to treat them as the adults that they are'.

An increasing number of churches are holding occasional special services geared to the mentally handicapped. Often these are associated with the annual Mencap week. How do ministers tackle this special 'gearing'?

The Revd. Phyllis Cordon, retired URC minister at Painswick, conducted a number of these Mencap services. She writes:

'I judge that, to have any success in contacts with these special people, it is necessary
    to have no fear of them
    to treat them as children, for they are, as we are, 'all God's children'
    to encourage them to participate in church services, but in a limited way, as perceived necessary
    never to be patronising
    to talk as to children (what adult does not secretly enjoy the children's bit in worship anyway?)

(It is, of course, a delicate path between talking as to children and being patronising. This minister is particularly good at relating to children too). For short talks in these services, Miss Cordon has made use of fairy stories, nursery rhymes, and a bunch of pansies with different faces.

John Stroud soon found in his hospital services that visual material and music (on tape) were important. Singing is popular, and music can be used to evoke feeling. He gave up reading Scripture, finding it more helpful to retell a parable. A theme proved helpful in getting them involved, talking about it.

When asked to take a Mencap service at his church, John decided to take the theme of Dragons. The Occupational Therapy department at the hospital had just made one, so the idea was familiar to some of the congregation. The dragon theme could be related to the problems of life, and to the Gospel story. The service was fast moving, divided into two minute sections, including a sketch, pictures on the overhead projector, and a dragon dance.

This year his theme was 'It's too big', with the action centring on the stories of David and Goliath, and little Zacchaeus.

The church liked the joy and exuberance of the mentally handicapped worshippers. The first approach had come from the Disabled Rights Group and the Hospital Friends. The move to repeat the service in subsequent years came from the congregation. There have been requests for such services more often. The minister feels this could be difficult to sustain, and they must think rather about integrating the handicapped into the normal life of the church.

At Loughborough the idea of a special service to reach out to the mentally handicapped arose through the work of their Link-Up Club. Some were worshipping regularly, but they decided last Christmas to invite the mentally handicapped and their families from all around to tea and the evening carol service. 250 attended the service, of whom about 100 were the handicapped and their families. The service included contributions from the handicapped: carols played on handbells, a recitation and a solo. The minister's talk was enlivened with glove puppets.

The leaders were aware of the risks of putting the handicapped 'on show', but it proved a moving and reverent service. The organist observed, 'I didn't know what to expect but felt the whole service to be one of delight'. A boy of thirteen commented, 'I wanted to cry. I don't know why, but I felt great and happy after'. Pat Maisch, the Link-Up leader, had doubts in advance: 'I had thought that it could turn into a form of entertainment and not a service of worship; that our normal congregation might stay away because of ignorance and fear of the mentally handicapped... I came away uplifted and thinking we've done it once, we can do it again. Why can't we think of our friends being with us on a more regular basis? ... The service was a success... but it only scratched the surface of what lies before us. The work has only just started and where do we go from here?'

A second service was held at Loughborough in June. The handbell ringers again took part, and a drama group acted, largely in mime, a story of a town cat (material from *Prudie finds out,* by Natania and Litza Jantz, Pandora Press, RKP). The minister, David Butcher, drew a brief message from this.

Each of the churches, whose special services feature here, are involved with the mentally handicapped in other caring ways. The services are highlights, which focus the work and provide opportunity to draw in more of the handicapped and their families, and to make the whole congregation more aware of the work being done. Their very success forbids a resting on laurels, but rather prompts further efforts in ministry that includes the mentally handicapped.

FAITH BOWERS

RESOURCES

There are many voluntary societies and self-help groups for parents and people with various types of mental handicap. Many such organisations have national headquarters and local branches.

It can be helpful for the minister to suggest or encourage contact with these bodies. They offer conversation with other people facing similar problems, interest in the special needs and advice on caring for the mentally handicapped person, sources of information, and sometimes practical help in areas like babysitting, short-term care, or lending books.

Trisha Dale, on behalf of the Baptist Union Working Group, has been gathering information on helpful organisations, residential care, and publications relating to mental handicap. These are listed below. She welcomes information on other such resources, and will be glad to supply information to anyone requiring it.

Some useful addresses:

British Epilepsy Association, New Wokingham Road, Wokingham, Berkshire

Down's Children's Association, 4 Oxford Street, London W1N 9FL (01 580 0511/2)

MENCAP (Royal Society for Mentally Handicapped Children and Adults), 123 Golden Lane, London EC1Y 0RT (01 253 9433)

National Association for Deaf/Blind and Rubella Handicapped, 311 Grays Inn Road, London WC1 (01 278 1009)

The Spastics Society, 12 Park Crescent, London W1 (01 636 5020)

Invalid Children's Aid Association, 126 Buckingham Palace Road, London SW1 (01730 9891)

The Group holds publications lists from the Associations of Professions for the Mentally Handicapped, British Institute of Mental Handicap, Campaign for Mentally Handicapped People, King's Fund Centre, and Mencap.

There is information about: Campaign for Mentally Handicapped People, Castle Priory College programme, Contact a Family, Enid Blyton Trust for Children (information centre and library for handicapped children), Family Link (Plumstead), Gatepost, Gateway Clubs, Independent Development Council for People with Mental Handicap, Intershare, King's Fund Centre, Mencap, National Autistic Society, National Children's Bureau, St Joseph's Centre.

On residential care, see the article following on Caresearch. Further information is held on: Association of Residential Committees for the Retarded, ARK Housing Association, Barvin Park, Camphill Village Trust, Catholic Handicapped Children's Fellowship, Christian Concern for the Mentally Handicapped, Cottage and Rural Enterprises, Elizabeth Fitzroy Homes, Guideposts Trust, Home Farm Trust, L'Arche, Larkfield Hall, MacIntyre, Purley Park Trust, St Elizabeth's - Much Hadham, Salter's Hill, Shaftesbury Society, Stallcombe House Farm, Wentwood Education, United Response.

A CARING COMPUTERISED INFORMATION SERVICE

Choosing a new home is almost always stressful. How much harder it must be to have the responsibility of finding a residential home for a mentally handicapped person. Caresearch has recently been set up to help simplify this task.

Caresearch is a computer-based information service designed to match the needs of a mentally handicapped client with the available places in residential homes. In order to do this, data on residential homes has been collected and is stored as a 'data base' in the computer. When a person needs residential care, their details are fed into the computer, and the addresses of suitable accommodation currently available come out in response. The data base can be constantly updated - an obvious advantage of a computer over a printed directory.

A typical request is for a place in a small unit, usually local. Jane Bayes of Caresearch says 'Everybody wants their own room in a town in nice small homes. People aren't looking for large country residences now, which is the way in which care for mentally handicapped people is changing'.

Anyone may use the service. So far most requests have come from the parents of mentally handicapped people, or their social workers, but there is no reason why ministers or other church leaders should not use Caresearch. The Questionnaire asks for basic details about the client's needs, classifying them as essential, preferred, and non-essential, to attempt as close a match between the mentally handicapped person and the available facilities as possible. Jane Bayes says that many parents find this a difficult concept to understand, and a mediator between the Caresearch form and the parents would be very helpful - a role a caring Christian leader could well fill.

Caresearch bridges the gap between not knowing anything of any residential homes and being inundated with information on many totally unsuitable homes. It can eliminate those in the wrong area, or with the wrong facilities or with no vacancies. Then it is up to the client's carer, parent or social worker, to contact the various possible homes for more information and to make the final choice.

Jane Bayes says that Caresearch has already successfully matched approximately two hundred people with residential care. About half of these have been for holiday accommodation: 'That's always a nice thing to do because there are a lot of homes that provide holiday accommodation'.

Caresearch shows the unfulfilled needs for residential care for mentally handicapped people too. A further four hundred people have applied to Caresearch, but for them no residential match has been possible. 'This is the other side of the coin. The cases that are very hard to place are the people with very severe problems who need long-term care. We're not finding them a home, because such homes do not exist. Caresearch can build up quite an interesting map of areas of care, and areas of need. We can back it up when someone says, "There just isn't anywhere for an aggressive physically handicapped mentally handicapped person." We can say that we've had forty people try to find a place, and it really is needed - look through our data base'.

Caresearch has been set up by United Response, which is a non-denominational Christian charity which runs homes for mentally handicapped adults in England. The computer was provided by the Department of Trade and Industry through the Information Technology Awareness Programme, and the staff are funded through the Manpower Services Commission. Caresearch has sought to give priority for these jobs to disabled people, and a spin-off of the scheme has been the training of some otherwise unemployed young people, including three who had a history of mental illness.

Caresearch, 1 Thorpe Close, Portobello Green. London W10
Telephone: 01 960 5666.

TRISHA DALE

AS YOU TRULY ARE

Create - not only in the beginning
each continues to
but WHAT?
We created you
through love for each other.
A seed of love
born to be loved
- yet imperfect?
In the world's eyes
- and, Yes, in ours
though NOT in God's.
But we love you
for you show us God's love
That we should try to be
with you and all people,
as God is with us.
Patient, tolerant,
understanding, firm,
yet truly loving.
Perfect or imperfect
you give us hope.
For one day
we shall fully realise
the Goal of God's creating love.
See you and all men
as you truly are -
A daughter, not only of ours,
but of God's.
Lovely and Loved!

PAT BATTARBEE

BIBLIOGRAPHY

A Guide for Chaplains serving in hospitals for the mentally handicapped, Sheffield Regional Hospital Board booklet.

Anderson, Rachel, *Tim Walks,* CIO, 1985. A children's book.

Anonymous, 'Handicapped but Human', *Family,* December 1981

Bayley, Michael, *The Local Church and Mentally Handicapped People,* CIO, 1984

Bicknell, Joan, 'Mentally Handicapped People in the Community: a challenge for the Church', *Crucible,* Oct-Dec 1983

Bradford, John, *Preparing the Mentally Handicapped for Confirmation,* Church of England Children's Society, 1981

Church of England Board for Social Responsibility, Committee for Social Work and Social Services:

No.69	May 1979	The Handicapped and Personal Relationships
84	Sept 1980	The Jay Report
87	Dec 1980	International Year of Disabled People
91	Apr 1981	Residential Establishments and the Parish
92	May 1981	? A Disabled Church
99	Dec 1981	Spiritual Rights
109	Oct 1982	Mentally Handicapped People and the Church's Response

Clifford, Stephanie, *Called to Belong: Preparing the Mentally Handicapped Person for Confirmation,* Kevin Mayhew, 1984

Duncan, Leslie H., *How shall we care? Helping children with severe learning difficulties,* Saint Andrew's Press, Edinburgh, 1980

Goss, Martin, *Mentally Handicapped People and the Churches: responding in Devon,* Council for Christian Care, Exeter, 1984 Leaflet

Hebden, Joan, *She'll never do anything, dear,* Human Horizons, 1985

HMSO, *The Education of Children in Hospitals for the Mentally Handicapped,* 1978

International Year of the Disabled Report, *Disabled People in the Church,* 1981

McGing, Katie, 'The Birth of a Mentally Handicapped Child', *All People* 27, July 1984

Miles, Michael, *Christianity and the Mentally Handicapped,* Christian Brethren Research Fellowship, Occasional Paper No.7, 1982

Oswin, Maureen, *Bereavement and Mentally Handicapped People,* Dec.1981, King's Fund Centre

Philps, Caroline, *Elizabeth Joy: a mother's story: the pain and joy of a Down's baby,* Lion, 1984

Potter, David, 'Handicapped Adults: a parent's dilemma', *Family,* October 1980

Shearer, Ann, *Everybody's Ethics: What future for handicapped babies?* The Campaign for Mentally Handicapped People, 1984

Tongeman, Peter, 'I'm Dawn, what's your name?' *Family,* April 1983

Townsend, Anne, 'Right to Live', *Family,* November 1981

URC Ministry of Healing, *Church and Community Care for Mentally Handicapped People,* 1985. Leaflet

Voluntary Council for Handicapped Children, *Help Starts Here,* 1976

Walker, Nigel, *Involving Volunteers with Mentally Handicapped People,* 1983

Walker, Blitz and Howe, *The Campbell-Rudolph Steiner Schools,* 1983?

White, Paul, *One in a Hundred: A Community Based Mental Handicap Project,* Cambridge House and Talbot, 1984

Wilson, David, *I am with you: an introduction to the religious education of the mentally handicapped,* St Paul Publications, 1975

Wilson, David, 'Catechetics with mentally handicapped children', *RE Today,* Spring 1985

Young, Frances, *Face to Face,* Epworth, 1985